Managing Virtual Machines: Hypervisors, Snapshots, and Resource Allocation

James Relington

DEDICATION

To those who seek knowledge, inspiration, and new perspectives—
may this book be a companion on your journey, a spark for curiosity,
and a reminder that every page turned is a step toward discovery.

AKNOWLEDGEMENTS

I would like to express my deepest gratitude to everyone who contributed to the creation of this book. To my colleagues and mentors, your insights and expertise have been invaluable. A special thank you to my family and friends for their unwavering support and encouragement throughout this journey.

Introduction to Virtual Machines

Virtual machines (VMs) represent a key element in the evolution of modern computing, providing flexibility and efficiency for a wide range of IT operations. At their core, virtual machines allow users to run an entire operating system and applications in an isolated environment within a physical host. This technology simulates the functions of a physical computer, providing a virtualized hardware platform for software to execute. The concept of virtualization, which underpins the function of VMs, dates back to the early days of computing but has only gained widespread adoption in recent decades. The rise of virtual machines has revolutionized the way organizations manage their IT infrastructure, enabling more efficient resource utilization and simplifying complex tasks like testing, backup, and disaster recovery.

The process of creating a virtual machine begins with the installation of a hypervisor, which is software that manages and allocates the physical resources of the host system to the virtual environment. The hypervisor acts as a mediator between the host hardware and the virtual machines running on it, allowing each VM to operate independently with its own virtualized CPU, memory, storage, and network interfaces. By abstracting the underlying physical resources, the hypervisor creates an environment in which VMs can run various operating systems and applications, often different from the host system's OS. This flexibility is a defining characteristic of virtual machines and is a major factor in their adoption across industries.

One of the most significant advantages of virtual machines is their ability to consolidate physical resources. Traditionally, each application or service required its own dedicated hardware, resulting in underutilization of computing resources. Virtualization allows multiple virtual machines to run on a single physical machine, each acting as if it is running on its own dedicated hardware. This consolidation reduces the need for physical servers, leading to cost savings, reduced power consumption, and lower data center space requirements. By running multiple VMs on a single host, organizations can achieve greater efficiency and scalability in managing their infrastructure.

The ability to isolate virtual machines from one another is another critical feature of VMs. Each virtual machine operates in a sandboxed environment, meaning that the actions performed within one VM have no direct impact on others. This isolation not only enhances security by preventing malicious software from affecting other VMs but also enables developers and system administrators to experiment with different configurations, operating systems, or software without the risk of corrupting the host system or other virtual environments. In a development or testing scenario, virtual machines provide a safe space to try out new ideas and configurations, ensuring that any issues encountered can be contained and resolved without affecting the broader infrastructure.

Furthermore, virtual machines offer significant flexibility in resource management. Virtual machines can be provisioned and decommissioned quickly, making it easier to scale infrastructure up or down based on changing needs. This is particularly beneficial in dynamic environments, such as cloud computing, where workloads may fluctuate throughout the day or week. Virtualization also allows for better resource allocation, ensuring that each VM is provided with the necessary amount of CPU power, memory, and storage to perform efficiently. This fine-grained control over resource allocation ensures that the host system remains responsive and that virtual machines can run demanding applications without causing bottlenecks or other performance issues.

The use of snapshots is another feature that adds to the appeal of virtual machines. A snapshot is a point-in-time copy of a VM's state, including its disk, memory, and configuration. Snapshots provide a quick way to capture the current state of a VM, which can be reverted to later if necessary. This is especially valuable for testing and development purposes, as it allows users to experiment with different configurations and changes without the fear of permanent damage. If a change leads to unexpected results or system failures, reverting to a previous snapshot restores the VM to its prior state, minimizing downtime and preventing data loss.

In addition to testing and development, virtual machines play a crucial role in disaster recovery. The ability to take snapshots or create full backups of virtual machines enables rapid restoration of services in the event of a hardware failure or system crash. Since VMs are typically hardware-independent, they can be moved or restored to a different host machine without compatibility issues, ensuring that critical applications can continue to run even in the face of infrastructure failures. This capability has made virtual machines an integral part of business continuity planning, where uptime and reliability are paramount.

Despite the many benefits, virtual machines are not without their challenges. The performance overhead introduced by virtualization can sometimes lead to inefficiencies, particularly when running resource-intensive applications. Hypervisors must balance the allocation of physical resources between the host and multiple virtual machines, and this can lead to contention for CPU, memory, or I/O resources. Although modern hypervisors are highly optimized to reduce this overhead, it is still something that needs to be carefully managed, especially in large-scale environments with numerous VMs.

Moreover, managing a virtualized environment can become complex as the number of virtual machines grows. Administrators must ensure that each VM is properly configured, secure, and maintained, while also overseeing the underlying physical infrastructure. In large organizations or cloud environments, this can require specialized tools and strategies to monitor VM performance, track resource usage, and perform tasks like VM migration and load balancing. Without the right tools and practices in place, virtualized environments can quickly become disorganized and difficult to manage.

The growing popularity of virtual machines has also led to the development of related technologies, such as containerization, which offers some of the same benefits but with different trade-offs. Containers provide a lightweight alternative to virtual machines by isolating applications at the process level rather than through full hardware emulation. While containers are often faster and more efficient than VMs, they do not offer the same level of isolation and flexibility, making virtual machines the preferred choice for many use cases, particularly where full operating system support and resource allocation are required.

In conclusion, virtual machines have transformed the way organizations manage their IT resources, providing unprecedented flexibility, efficiency, and scalability. They have become a cornerstone of modern IT infrastructure, enabling everything from testing and development to cloud computing and disaster recovery. While there are challenges associated with virtualization, the benefits far outweigh the drawbacks, making virtual machines an essential tool for businesses and developers alike. As the technology continues to evolve, virtual machines are likely to remain at the forefront of innovation in computing.

Understanding Hypervisors: Types and Functions

A hypervisor is a critical component in the world of virtualization, serving as the intermediary between the physical hardware of a host machine and the virtual machines (VMs) that run on it. It is the software layer responsible for managing the allocation of resources to VMs, ensuring that each VM operates as if it has its own dedicated hardware. Hypervisors play a central role in enabling virtualization by abstracting the physical hardware, allowing multiple VMs to run independently on the same physical system. Understanding the different types of hypervisors and their functions is essential for anyone involved in managing or designing virtualized environments.

There are two primary types of hypervisors: Type 1 and Type 2. Each type has its own unique characteristics, and they differ primarily in how they interact with the host system's hardware and operating systems. Type 1 hypervisors, also known as bare-metal hypervisors, run directly on the physical hardware of a machine without relying on a host operating system. Because they interact directly with the hardware, Type 1 hypervisors tend to offer better performance and greater stability compared to Type 2 hypervisors. They are typically used in enterprise environments, data centers, and cloud infrastructures where performance, scalability, and security are crucial. Type 1 hypervisors often provide more robust management capabilities, including tools for handling large numbers of VMs and advanced features such as live migration, VM snapshots, and resource scheduling.

In contrast, Type 2 hypervisors, also known as hosted hypervisors, run on top of an existing operating system. Rather than interfacing directly with the hardware, Type 2 hypervisors rely on the host OS to manage hardware resources. This additional layer of abstraction introduces some overhead, which can lead to performance degradation when compared to Type 1 hypervisors. However, Type 2 hypervisors are typically easier to install and configure, making them a popular choice for desktop virtualization or smaller-scale environments. They are ideal for use cases where the hypervisor is needed for isolated testing, development, or running virtual machines on personal computers. Examples of Type 2 hypervisors include VirtualBox, VMware Workstation, and Parallels Desktop.

The function of a hypervisor is centered around resource allocation and management. The hypervisor allocates physical resources such as CPU, memory, storage, and network interfaces to the virtual machines running on the host. It ensures that each VM has access to the resources it needs to operate efficiently, while also preventing VMs from interfering with each other. The hypervisor is responsible for isolating VMs from each other, ensuring that each VM operates in its own virtualized environment. This isolation not only enhances security by preventing one VM from impacting the performance or stability of another, but also allows for greater flexibility in configuring and running different operating systems and applications on the same physical machine.

Another important function of a hypervisor is virtualization of hardware resources. When a VM is created, the hypervisor allocates virtual hardware to it, including virtual CPUs, memory, storage devices, and network adapters. These virtual components are mapped to the physical resources of the host system by the hypervisor, allowing the VM to function as though it were running on a physical machine. The virtual hardware provided to the VM may not necessarily match the exact specifications of the physical hardware, but it is designed to provide the necessary functionality for the guest operating system and applications. This abstraction allows for greater flexibility in managing resources and enables VMs to run on a variety of hardware platforms without compatibility issues.

One of the key features of hypervisors is their ability to manage multiple virtual machines simultaneously. Hypervisors provide mechanisms for scheduling and balancing the allocation of resources across the VMs, ensuring that each one receives its fair share of CPU time, memory, and other resources. This is particularly important in environments with a large number of VMs, where resource contention can become an issue. Advanced hypervisors offer features such as dynamic resource allocation, where the hypervisor can automatically adjust the resources allocated to VMs based on current usage patterns, ensuring that performance is optimized across the system. This flexibility is a significant advantage of virtualization, as it allows for more efficient utilization of physical resources and improves overall system performance.

In addition to resource management, hypervisors provide mechanisms for monitoring and controlling virtual machines. They include tools for managing VM lifecycle operations such as creation, suspension, migration, and deletion. Hypervisors also provide performance monitoring capabilities, allowing administrators to track the resource usage of individual VMs and the host system. This monitoring can help identify bottlenecks or performance issues and ensure that resources are being used efficiently. Advanced hypervisors may offer features like real-time performance analysis, where administrators can track the performance of VMs in real time and make adjustments as needed to ensure optimal operation.

Hypervisors also play an important role in ensuring the security of virtualized environments. The isolation provided by the hypervisor prevents VMs from accessing or affecting the resources of other VMs, reducing the risk of security breaches. Hypervisors also include features to enhance VM security, such as secure boot mechanisms, which ensure that only trusted code is executed in the virtual environment. Some hypervisors also support features like encrypted virtual machines, where the data stored in the VM's virtual disk is encrypted to prevent unauthorized access. These security features make hypervisors an essential component of secure virtualization infrastructures, especially in environments where sensitive data is being processed or stored.

Another important function of hypervisors is the ability to support VM migration. In a virtualized environment, it is often necessary to move virtual machines from one physical host to another, either for load balancing, maintenance, or disaster recovery purposes. Hypervisors enable live migration, where a running VM can be moved from one host to another without downtime. This is achieved by transferring the VM's memory, storage, and other state information between the hosts while the VM continues to run. Live migration is a powerful feature in large-scale virtualized environments, allowing administrators to optimize resource utilization and ensure high availability of services.

The role of hypervisors in cloud computing cannot be overstated. In cloud environments, hypervisors enable the creation and management of virtualized instances, which can be rapidly provisioned, scaled, and decommissioned based on demand. Hypervisors are a fundamental part of the infrastructure-as-a-service (IaaS) model, where users can deploy and manage virtual machines in the cloud without having to worry about the underlying physical hardware. Cloud providers rely on hypervisors to deliver the flexibility, scalability, and resource management capabilities required for modern cloud computing environments.

The ongoing development of hypervisor technology has led to improvements in performance, security, and management capabilities.

As the demand for virtualization continues to grow, hypervisors are evolving to meet the needs of increasingly complex IT infrastructures. Advances in hypervisor design, including support for containerization and improved integration with cloud environments, are shaping the future of virtualization and enabling new use cases and capabilities. The importance of hypervisors in virtualization cannot be understated, as they provide the foundation for modern IT infrastructures, allowing organizations to maximize resource utilization, increase flexibility, and enhance security.

The Evolution of Virtualization Technology

The evolution of virtualization technology is a fascinating journey that spans several decades, shaping the way modern IT infrastructures are designed and managed. From its early conceptual stages to the highly sophisticated platforms of today, virtualization has undergone significant transformations that have enabled organizations to maximize their computing resources and streamline operations. At its core, virtualization allows for the creation of virtual instances of physical hardware, enabling the running of multiple operating systems and applications on a single physical machine. This technology has evolved from a niche solution used primarily in large data centers to a mainstream tool that powers everything from personal computing to cloud infrastructure.

Virtualization began in the 1960s with early attempts to partition mainframe computers into multiple virtual machines. IBM was at the forefront of this innovation, introducing the concept of virtual machines on their mainframe systems. The idea was simple: create the ability to run multiple workloads on a single physical machine, each with its own isolated environment. IBM's mainframe systems used virtualization to enable efficient sharing of computing resources, allowing different departments within large organizations to run their applications on the same machine without interference. Early forms of virtualization were quite rudimentary, with limited capabilities and performance constraints. However, this laid the foundation for the future of virtualization, establishing the idea of resource abstraction and isolation.

During the 1970s and 1980s, virtualization technology remained largely confined to the mainframe world. While there were some attempts to apply virtualization concepts to smaller, less powerful computers, the technology did not gain significant traction outside of the enterprise environment. The primary reason for this was the sheer cost and complexity of implementing virtualization. Hardware was expensive, and the computing power available at the time was far from sufficient to support the kind of virtualization that would be required for widespread use. It wasn't until the advent of more powerful and affordable hardware in the 1990s that virtualization began to gain mainstream interest.

The 1990s marked a significant turning point in the evolution of virtualization. The development of x86 architecture, which became the dominant architecture for personal computers, created new possibilities for virtualization. Unlike previous generations of hardware, which were designed primarily for single-task, monolithic operations, x86 processors were more flexible and capable of supporting virtualized environments. In the late 1990s, VMware emerged as a key player in the virtualization space, creating the first commercial x86 hypervisor. This innovation made it possible to run multiple virtual machines on standard desktop computers, providing unprecedented flexibility for developers, testers, and administrators. VMware's products were initially used to improve server utilization and reduce hardware costs, but as the technology matured, virtualization began to find its way into a broader range of use cases, including disaster recovery, testing and development, and application isolation.

As the 2000s progressed, virtualization technology continued to evolve rapidly. The early barriers to widespread adoption—such as cost, performance, and complexity—were gradually overcome with advancements in hardware and software. One of the most significant developments during this time was the introduction of hardware-assisted virtualization. Intel and AMD, two of the largest semiconductor manufacturers, introduced processor extensions specifically designed to enhance virtualization performance. These extensions, such as Intel VT-x and AMD-V, allowed the hypervisor to execute operations with greater efficiency and reduced overhead, improving the performance of virtual machines. This shift to hardware-assisted virtualization was a game-changer, as it made virtualization more accessible and efficient for a wide range of applications.

At the same time, the growing demand for cloud computing services helped accelerate the development of virtualization technologies. The rise of cloud providers such as Amazon Web Services (AWS), Microsoft Azure, and Google Cloud demonstrated the immense potential of virtualized environments to support scalable, on-demand computing. Virtualization became a cornerstone of cloud infrastructure, enabling providers to quickly provision, scale, and manage resources for customers. Virtual machines (VMs) became the building blocks of cloud computing, providing the flexibility to run diverse workloads on shared physical infrastructure. The ability to create, destroy, and migrate VMs with minimal downtime enabled cloud providers to offer highly elastic and cost-effective services, transforming the IT landscape in the process.

As virtualization became more entrenched in cloud environments, the next phase of its evolution involved the refinement of tools and management platforms. Virtualization management solutions like VMware vSphere, Microsoft Hyper-V, and open-source platforms like KVM and Xen provided administrators with sophisticated ways to manage large-scale virtual environments. These platforms offered features such as live migration, high availability, and automated provisioning, which were essential for maintaining uptime and ensuring optimal resource allocation. Additionally, the integration of virtualization with other technologies, such as containers and software-defined networking (SDN), led to the development of more flexible and dynamic infrastructure models. Virtualization management platforms became essential for managing complex hybrid and multi-cloud environments, where workloads were distributed across different cloud providers and on-premises data centers.

The most recent stage in the evolution of virtualization has seen the rise of containerization, a lightweight alternative to traditional virtual machines. Containers, such as those based on Docker and Kubernetes, provide a more efficient method of isolating applications and workloads compared to full virtualization. Unlike virtual machines, which require a full operating system to run, containers package only the application and its dependencies, making them smaller and faster to deploy. Containers share the host operating system's kernel, reducing the overhead associated with running multiple isolated instances. While containers and virtual machines serve different purposes, they are increasingly being used together in modern IT environments. Containers are often used for microservices and application-level isolation, while virtual machines continue to provide the full isolation required for running complete operating systems and complex workloads.

The continuous development of virtualization technology has brought with it improvements in performance, security, and scalability. Virtualization is no longer just a tool for optimizing hardware usage; it has become a foundational technology for modern IT infrastructures. As virtualization has evolved, it has become deeply integrated into everything from private data centers to public cloud platforms, enabling greater flexibility, faster provisioning, and more efficient resource management. The rise of technologies like container orchestration, serverless computing, and edge computing all rely on the underlying principles of virtualization. Virtualization's ability to abstract resources, isolate workloads, and improve resource utilization has made it an essential tool for organizations of all sizes, across a wide range of industries.

The evolution of virtualization technology continues to shape the future of computing, and as hardware becomes more powerful and software more sophisticated, virtualization is poised to remain a key driver of innovation. The technology's ability to provide scalable, cost-effective, and secure solutions is more important than ever in today's rapidly changing IT landscape. With the ongoing advancements in hardware, software, and cloud services, virtualization is expected to continue evolving, unlocking new possibilities for managing and deploying IT resources more efficiently.

How Virtual Machines Interact with Host Systems

Virtual machines (VMs) are a cornerstone of modern computing, enabling multiple independent environments to run on a single physical host system. The interaction between a virtual machine and its host system is fundamental to how virtualization works. At the core of this interaction lies the hypervisor, a piece of software that manages and coordinates the virtual resources used by VMs. Virtual machines rely on the host system's physical resources, such as the CPU, memory, storage, and network interfaces, to operate, while the hypervisor ensures that these resources are shared and allocated appropriately among the VMs.

When a virtual machine is created, it is essentially a software emulation of a physical computer. Each VM is provided with virtualized hardware components, such as virtual CPUs, virtual memory, and virtual storage devices, that allow it to run an operating system and applications just like a physical machine. These virtualized components are mapped by the hypervisor to the underlying physical hardware of the host system, but the VM itself does not directly interact with the host's physical hardware. Instead, the hypervisor acts as an intermediary, controlling the communication between the VM and the host system.

The process begins when a virtual machine is initialized. The hypervisor allocates a portion of the physical resources from the host system to the VM, including CPU cycles, RAM, and disk space. This allocation is managed based on the VM's configured specifications and the overall resource availability of the host system. For example, when the VM requests CPU resources, the hypervisor will schedule CPU time for the VM based on the host's current load, ensuring that each VM receives a fair share of processing power. Similarly, when a VM needs access to memory, the hypervisor manages the mapping of virtual memory pages to the physical memory of the host system, providing the VM with the memory it requires without allowing it to access memory allocated to other VMs or the host itself.

A key feature of the interaction between a virtual machine and the host system is the abstraction of physical hardware. The VM does not need to be aware of the specific hardware details of the host system, such as the type of processor, storage devices, or network interfaces. The hypervisor abstracts these details, presenting the VM with a consistent virtualized environment regardless of the underlying hardware. This abstraction allows for greater flexibility, as VMs can be moved between different host systems with varying hardware configurations without requiring reconfiguration of the virtual machine itself. The virtual hardware that the hypervisor provides to the VM is typically designed to be hardware-independent, meaning that the guest operating system running inside the VM does not need to know or care about the specifics of the physical hardware.

The virtual network interfaces within the VM are another example of how virtual machines interact with the host system. VMs typically have one or more virtual network adapters that allow them to communicate with other VMs and with external networks, such as the internet. The hypervisor creates a virtual network bridge that connects the virtual network adapters of the VMs to the host's physical network interfaces. This enables the VMs to send and receive data through the host system's network interface, effectively isolating the virtual machines from the physical network infrastructure. The hypervisor may also provide additional network features, such as virtual switches, firewalls, and network address translation (NAT), to manage traffic between the VMs and the outside world.

Storage is another critical aspect of how virtual machines interact with the host system. When a VM is created, the hypervisor allocates a virtual disk for the VM, which is essentially a file stored on the host's physical storage. This virtual disk is typically managed by the hypervisor and appears to the guest operating system as a regular hard drive. The hypervisor maps the VM's storage requests to the host's physical storage, ensuring that data is read from and written to the correct location. Virtual machines may also use shared storage, where multiple VMs access the same storage device, or they may use separate storage for each VM, depending on the configuration. In cloud environments or enterprise data centers, shared storage is often used to enable features like live migration, where a VM is moved from one host to another without downtime.

While virtual machines are isolated from each other and from the host system, they do interact with the host in several important ways. The hypervisor ensures that each VM's resources are managed and protected, but it also provides mechanisms for the host system to monitor and control the virtual machines. For example, the host system can monitor the resource usage of each VM, track performance metrics, and even intervene in the event of resource contention or performance issues. If a VM is consuming too many resources or misbehaving, the hypervisor can throttle its resource usage or suspend the VM to prevent it from affecting other VMs on the same host. The hypervisor also enables live migration of VMs, where a running VM can be moved from one host to another, allowing for load balancing and maintenance without interrupting the VM's operation.

Another important aspect of the interaction between virtual machines and host systems is the handling of device passthrough. In some cases, virtual machines need direct access to specific physical devices, such as a graphics card or network interface card (NIC). The hypervisor can enable device passthrough, where a physical device is made directly available to a VM. This allows the VM to use the device as if it were physically installed in the VM itself. Device passthrough is commonly used in high-performance scenarios, such as virtualized gaming, video rendering, or network-intensive applications, where the VM needs to access specific hardware resources to perform optimally.

Virtual machines also interact with the host system in terms of system state and management. For instance, when the host system needs to be rebooted for maintenance or updates, the hypervisor ensures that the VMs are either paused, saved, or migrated to other hosts. Similarly, the host system manages the overall lifecycle of the VMs, including their creation, suspension, resumption, and deletion. Virtualization management platforms provide administrators with tools to manage these interactions efficiently, often allowing for automated VM provisioning, monitoring, and scaling based on resource demands.

The relationship between a virtual machine and its host system is dynamic and involves continuous coordination by the hypervisor. The hypervisor's role as an intermediary ensures that the virtualized environment remains stable, secure, and efficient. This interaction between the VM and the host system is what enables virtualization to provide the flexibility, isolation, and resource management needed for modern IT environments. Whether for personal use, development, testing, or enterprise-level applications, the seamless interaction between virtual machines and their host systems forms the backbone of virtualization technology.

Benefits and Drawbacks of Virtual Machines

Virtual machines (VMs) have become a cornerstone of modern computing, offering flexibility, resource optimization, and ease of management for IT infrastructures. Their ability to run multiple operating systems on a single physical machine has revolutionized the way organizations approach computing, providing significant benefits in terms of resource efficiency, scalability, and isolation. However, as with any technology, virtual machines also come with their own set of challenges and limitations. Understanding both the benefits and drawbacks of virtual machines is crucial for anyone considering their adoption, whether in a small development environment or a large enterprise data center.

One of the primary benefits of virtual machines is resource consolidation. Traditionally, each physical server would run a single operating system and application, often leading to underutilization of hardware resources. Virtual machines allow multiple operating systems and applications to run on a single physical server, each in its own isolated environment. This consolidation reduces the need for additional physical hardware, leading to cost savings in terms of both capital expenditures and operational costs such as power, cooling, and space. In large data centers, this ability to consolidate resources can result in significant savings and a more efficient use of available infrastructure.

Along with resource consolidation, virtual machines enable greater flexibility in managing workloads. VMs can be easily provisioned, cloned, and migrated across different physical hosts without significant downtime. This flexibility is particularly advantageous in cloud computing environments, where workloads may need to be rapidly scaled up or down based on demand. Virtualization allows for the dynamic allocation of resources, meaning that VMs can be adjusted to meet changing workload requirements. For instance, if a particular application or service needs more CPU or memory, resources can be reallocated from other VMs or hosts, ensuring optimal performance without the need for physical hardware upgrades.

Another significant advantage of virtual machines is their ability to provide isolation. Each virtual machine operates as an independent environment, with its own virtualized hardware, operating system, and applications. This isolation ensures that the actions of one VM do not affect others. For example, if one VM experiences a crash or is compromised by malicious software, it will not impact other VMs running on the same host system. This isolation is particularly useful in multi-tenant environments, such as public cloud platforms, where each tenant may be running their own set of applications or services. The ability to isolate workloads enhances security by preventing cross-VM vulnerabilities and ensuring that sensitive data remains protected.

Virtual machines also offer advantages in terms of disaster recovery and business continuity. Because VMs are abstracted from the underlying hardware, they can be easily backed up, replicated, and restored. Snapshots of VMs can be taken at any point in time, allowing for quick recovery in case of a system failure or data loss. Furthermore, virtual machines can be migrated from one physical host to another, either for maintenance purposes or in the event of hardware failure. This ability to move VMs between hosts without downtime ensures that critical applications and services remain available, even in the face of infrastructure issues.

In development and testing environments, virtual machines offer significant benefits. Developers and testers can create isolated environments to test new applications, configurations, or updates without affecting production systems. If an issue arises during testing, the VM can be reverted to a previous snapshot, eliminating the need for lengthy troubleshooting or reinstallation of software. This ability to create and manage multiple test environments on a single machine greatly speeds up development cycles and reduces the overhead associated with managing separate physical test systems.

Despite these numerous advantages, virtual machines are not without their drawbacks. One of the main disadvantages of using VMs is the performance overhead associated with virtualization. While modern hypervisors are highly optimized, there is still some level of resource overhead that comes with running multiple VMs on a single physical host. The hypervisor itself consumes CPU and memory resources, and each virtual machine requires its own operating system, which adds additional layers of abstraction. As a result, VMs may not perform as efficiently as running applications directly on physical hardware. This overhead can become particularly noticeable in resource-intensive applications, such as high-performance computing, gaming, or large-scale data processing, where physical hardware is typically more suitable.

Another drawback of virtual machines is the complexity involved in managing large virtualized environments. While virtualization provides many benefits in terms of resource allocation and flexibility, it also introduces additional layers of management and monitoring. Administrators must ensure that each VM is properly configured, secure, and maintained, while also overseeing the performance of the host system and ensuring that resources are being allocated efficiently. In large environments with many VMs, this can become a significant challenge, requiring specialized tools and expertise. Without proper management, a virtualized environment can quickly become disorganized, leading to inefficiencies and potential security risks.

In terms of storage, virtual machines also present some challenges. Each VM typically requires its own virtual disk, which is stored as a file on the host system. While this allows for easy management and backup of VM storage, it can lead to inefficiencies when running a large number of VMs. The underlying physical storage system must be able to handle the demands of multiple virtual machines, and without proper planning, storage performance can degrade. Additionally, because VMs rely on the host's physical storage, there is always a risk of data loss or corruption if the host system experiences failure, particularly if backup and redundancy measures are not in place.

Security can also be a concern when using virtual machines, particularly in multi-tenant environments. While VMs are isolated from one another, vulnerabilities can still arise in the hypervisor itself or through misconfigurations. A compromised hypervisor could potentially allow an attacker to escape from one VM and gain access to others running on the same host. Similarly, if a VM is misconfigured or lacks proper security measures, it could become an entry point for attackers to exploit vulnerabilities in the underlying infrastructure. While virtualization does provide a layer of isolation, it is not a substitute for proper security practices and controls, which are essential to maintaining the integrity of virtualized environments.

Finally, virtual machines can present challenges when it comes to licensing and compliance. Running multiple instances of an operating system or application on a single physical host may require additional licensing, depending on the terms of the software vendor's agreements. This can lead to increased costs, particularly for organizations running large numbers of VMs. In addition, ensuring compliance with industry regulations or internal policies can be more complex in a virtualized environment, as administrators must account for the management and security of both physical and virtual resources.

Virtual machines provide many advantages, including resource consolidation, flexibility, isolation, and improved disaster recovery. These benefits make them an essential tool in modern IT infrastructure, particularly in cloud computing, development, and testing environments. However, they also come with performance overhead, increased complexity, storage challenges, and security concerns. Understanding both the benefits and drawbacks of virtual machines is critical for organizations seeking to optimize their IT resources and ensure that virtualization technology is implemented effectively and securely. As the technology continues to evolve, it will likely address many of these challenges, further enhancing the value of virtual machines in various computing environments.

In-depth Look at Type 1 Hypervisors

Type 1 hypervisors, also known as bare-metal hypervisors, are a central component of modern virtualization technology. Unlike Type 2 hypervisors, which run on top of an existing operating system, Type 1 hypervisors are installed directly on the physical hardware of a host machine, effectively replacing the need for an underlying operating system. This architecture gives Type 1 hypervisors several distinct advantages, including better performance, enhanced security, and greater stability. To understand their significance in virtualization, it is essential to explore the characteristics, architecture, and use cases of Type 1 hypervisors.

The primary function of a Type 1 hypervisor is to manage and allocate the physical resources of the host system, such as CPU, memory, storage, and network interfaces, to the virtual machines (VMs) that run on it. Each VM runs its own operating system and applications, with the hypervisor providing an isolated and virtualized environment. The hypervisor acts as an intermediary between the VMs and the underlying hardware, ensuring that each VM has access to the necessary resources while preventing interference between VMs. This direct interaction with the hardware allows Type 1 hypervisors to operate with minimal overhead, providing superior performance compared to Type 2 hypervisors.

One of the key advantages of Type 1 hypervisors is their efficiency. Because they do not rely on a host operating system, they can dedicate more system resources to the virtual machines themselves. In Type 2 hypervisors, the host operating system consumes some of the resources, leaving less available for the virtualized environments. With a Type 1 hypervisor, the resources are allocated directly to the VMs, ensuring that they receive the optimal performance for their workloads. This is particularly important in environments where resource-intensive applications or large-scale virtualized infrastructures are being run, such as in enterprise data centers or cloud computing platforms.

The architecture of a Type 1 hypervisor is designed to be lightweight and highly optimized. These hypervisors typically have a small codebase, which reduces the potential for bugs or vulnerabilities. The absence of a host operating system also eliminates the need for additional layers of software management, making the hypervisor more efficient and secure. Because of their direct interaction with hardware, Type 1 hypervisors can make better use of modern hardware capabilities, such as hardware-assisted virtualization, which further improves performance. This is one reason why Type 1 hypervisors are commonly used in high-performance environments, such as cloud computing, where large numbers of VMs need to be managed and provisioned quickly.

Security is another significant benefit of Type 1 hypervisors. Since these hypervisors run directly on the physical hardware, they have greater control over the system's resources and are less susceptible to vulnerabilities that might affect a host operating system. In a Type 1 hypervisor, the hypervisor itself is isolated from the virtual machines, providing a higher level of security. The hypervisor controls access to the host system's resources, ensuring that VMs cannot interfere with each other or the host system. This isolation is especially important in multi-tenant environments, where different organizations may be running their VMs on the same physical infrastructure. By using a Type 1 hypervisor, organizations can ensure that the workloads of one tenant do not impact the security or stability of another tenant's workloads.

Another advantage of Type 1 hypervisors is their scalability. These hypervisors are designed to manage large numbers of virtual machines, making them ideal for enterprise environments where scalability is a critical requirement. In cloud computing platforms and virtualized data centers, Type 1 hypervisors are used to create and manage thousands of virtual machines, often running a variety of operating systems and applications. These hypervisors provide powerful management tools that allow administrators to monitor, provision, and allocate resources to virtual machines efficiently. With features like live migration, load balancing, and resource scheduling, Type 1 hypervisors make it easier to scale virtualized environments based on changing workloads.

Type 1 hypervisors also provide better fault tolerance and high availability. Many enterprise-grade Type 1 hypervisors include built-in features that ensure the availability of virtual machines in the event of a failure. For example, if a physical host fails, the virtual machines running on that host can be automatically migrated to other hosts in the cluster, ensuring minimal downtime and continued access to services. This feature is essential in mission-critical applications, where downtime is not acceptable. High availability is particularly important in industries such as finance, healthcare, and telecommunications, where continuous uptime is crucial for business operations.

While Type 1 hypervisors offer many advantages, they are not without their challenges. One of the primary drawbacks of Type 1 hypervisors is the complexity of setup and management. Since Type 1 hypervisors operate without an underlying operating system, administrators must have a deep understanding of hardware, networking, and virtualization concepts to deploy and maintain these systems effectively. Additionally, while Type 1 hypervisors are highly efficient, they may not be as user-friendly as Type 2 hypervisors, which typically offer more straightforward installation and configuration processes. This can make Type 1 hypervisors less appealing for small-scale environments or individual users who do not have the technical expertise to manage complex virtualization platforms.

Furthermore, while Type 1 hypervisors are optimized for performance, they can be more resource-intensive when running multiple VMs on a single physical host. The more virtual machines that are created, the greater the demand on the physical host's resources, including CPU, memory, and storage. To address this, organizations must ensure that they have sufficient hardware capacity to support the number of virtual machines required. This can lead to increased costs for purchasing and maintaining high-performance hardware. However, in large-scale data center environments, this cost is often offset by the benefits of virtualization, including the ability to consolidate resources and reduce hardware expenditures.

In terms of management, Type 1 hypervisors require specialized tools and software to monitor and control the virtualized environment. While these tools are generally more robust and powerful than those available for Type 2 hypervisors, they can also be complex and require a certain level of expertise to use effectively. In large environments with many virtual machines, managing the resources, ensuring security, and monitoring performance can be a daunting task without the proper tools in place.

Type 1 hypervisors are crucial to modern virtualization strategies, particularly in large-scale, high-performance environments. They offer significant benefits, including improved performance, enhanced security, scalability, and fault tolerance. These advantages make Type 1 hypervisors the preferred choice for enterprise data centers, cloud platforms, and other high-demand environments. While they come with challenges in terms of complexity and hardware requirements, the capabilities they provide in terms of resource management, isolation, and high availability make them indispensable for managing virtualized infrastructures at scale. The continued development of Type 1 hypervisors will likely bring even more advanced features and greater integration with emerging technologies, further cementing their role in the future of IT infrastructure.

In-depth Look at Type 2 Hypervisors

Type 2 hypervisors, also known as hosted hypervisors, are a critical component in the landscape of virtualization technology, offering a more flexible and accessible approach compared to their Type 1 counterparts. Unlike Type 1 hypervisors, which are installed directly on the physical hardware of a host system, Type 2 hypervisors run on top of an existing operating system. This difference in architecture gives Type 2 hypervisors several unique characteristics, such as ease of installation, broader compatibility, and the ability to leverage the host system's resources. However, this architecture also introduces certain limitations and challenges that can affect performance, scalability, and security. To understand the role of Type 2 hypervisors in virtualization, it is important to delve into their features, advantages, and limitations.

The core function of a Type 2 hypervisor is to create and manage virtual machines (VMs) on a host system. The hypervisor provides a virtualized environment for the VMs, abstracting the underlying hardware and allowing multiple operating systems to run concurrently on the same physical machine. Each virtual machine operates as an independent entity, with its own virtualized resources, such as CPU, memory, storage, and network interfaces. The hypervisor handles the communication between the VMs and the host system, ensuring that each VM has access to the necessary resources while preventing conflicts between them. The virtual machines may run different operating systems, allowing for a diverse range of applications and use cases on a single physical machine.

One of the key benefits of Type 2 hypervisors is their ease of installation and use. Because they run on top of an existing operating system, Type

2 hypervisors are typically much easier to install and configure than Type 1 hypervisors. Users do not need to worry about configuring hardware settings or managing a bare-metal hypervisor. Instead, they can install the Type 2 hypervisor just like any other software application, making it accessible to a broader audience, including home users, developers, and small businesses. The simplicity of installation and configuration makes Type 2 hypervisors an attractive option for those who need to run virtual machines for development, testing, or personal use without the complexity of enterprise-grade solutions.

Additionally, Type 2 hypervisors often provide a wide range of compatibility with different host operating systems. Whether the host system is running Windows, macOS, or Linux, Type 2 hypervisors can be installed and used to run virtual machines. This broad compatibility ensures that users can create and manage virtualized environments regardless of the underlying operating system of the host system. This flexibility makes Type 2 hypervisors ideal for developers who need to test software on multiple operating systems or for users who want to run different OSes for specific tasks, such as testing applications on different platforms.

Another advantage of Type 2 hypervisors is their ability to integrate well with the host operating system. Since they run on top of the host OS, they can take advantage of the host's native features, such as file management, security controls, and networking configurations. For example, a Type 2 hypervisor can access the host system's file system to create and manage virtual disks for VMs, making it easier to store and manage VM data. Similarly, networking configurations can be shared between the host and the virtual machines, allowing VMs to access the same network resources as the host system. This integration streamlines the process of managing virtualized environments, making it easier for users to configure and control their virtual machines.

While Type 2 hypervisors offer several advantages in terms of ease of use and compatibility, they also come with certain limitations that can affect their performance and scalability. One of the most significant drawbacks of Type 2 hypervisors is the overhead associated with running them on top of a host operating system. Since the hypervisor relies on the host OS to manage hardware resources, the performance of the virtual machines can be impacted by the additional layer of abstraction. The host operating system consumes resources, such as CPU and memory, which reduces the amount of available resources for the virtual machines. This can lead to slower performance, particularly in resource-intensive applications or when running multiple VMs on a single host. In contrast, Type 1 hypervisors, which run directly on the hardware, are able to allocate resources more efficiently, resulting in better performance and scalability.

The overhead introduced by the host operating system can also impact the scalability of Type 2 hypervisors. Since they rely on the host OS to manage resources, there is a limit to the number of virtual machines that can be efficiently run on a single physical machine. As the number of VMs increases, the host system may struggle to allocate sufficient resources, leading to performance degradation. This makes Type 2 hypervisors less suitable for large-scale virtualization environments, such as those found in data centers or cloud infrastructures. For such environments, Type 1 hypervisors are typically preferred, as they can handle a larger number of VMs with greater efficiency.

Security is another area where Type 2 hypervisors face challenges. Because they run on top of a host operating system, they are vulnerable to the same security risks that affect the host OS. If the host operating system is compromised, the hypervisor and the virtual machines running on it may also be at risk. Additionally, because Type 2 hypervisors rely on the host system for networking and storage, any security vulnerabilities in the host OS can potentially be exploited to gain unauthorized access to the virtual machines. In contrast, Type 1 hypervisors, which run directly on the hardware, are typically more secure because they are isolated from the host system's OS and are less susceptible to attacks targeting the host.

Type 2 hypervisors also require more resources to run compared to Type 1 hypervisors. Since they need the host OS to function, both the host system and the virtual machines share the available system resources, such as CPU, memory, and storage. In environments where performance is critical, such as in enterprise applications or high-performance computing, this shared resource model can create bottlenecks, affecting the overall efficiency of the system. Type 2 hypervisors are generally better suited for light workloads, development, and testing purposes, where resource demands are lower.

Despite these drawbacks, Type 2 hypervisors continue to be a popular choice for users who need virtualization on a smaller scale. They are especially useful in development and testing environments, where developers can quickly create and test applications across multiple platforms without the need for dedicated hardware for each operating system. Additionally, Type 2 hypervisors are commonly used for personal or hobbyist projects, where users need to run multiple operating systems on a single machine for various tasks, such as running Linux on a Windows or macOS host.

Type 2 hypervisors provide a practical solution for users who require virtualization in environments where performance and scalability are not the primary concerns. Their ease of installation, broad compatibility with different operating systems, and integration with the host system make them an ideal choice for individuals, small businesses, and developers. While they do have limitations in terms of resource overhead and security, Type 2 hypervisors remain a valuable tool for many use cases, offering a simple and effective way to create and manage virtual machines.

Virtual Machine Hardware Emulation

Virtual machine hardware emulation is one of the cornerstones of virtualization technology, enabling the creation of virtual environments that mimic the functionality of physical machines. When a virtual machine (VM) is created, it requires access to virtualized hardware resources such as CPU, memory, storage, and network interfaces. This is where hardware emulation comes into play. By abstracting the underlying physical hardware, virtual machine software, typically a hypervisor, is able to present an environment to the virtual machine that behaves much like a traditional physical system, even though it runs on shared, virtualized hardware. This process of emulation is crucial for allowing virtual machines to run operating systems and applications without the need for dedicated physical hardware for each instance.

Hardware emulation in virtual machines operates by providing the virtual machine with virtualized components that emulate the hardware features of a physical computer. The most important virtualized components include virtual CPUs, virtual memory, virtual network adapters, and virtual storage devices. These components are not physically separate from the host system but are created through software, enabling the VM to interact with the host's hardware as though it were running on a physical machine. The virtual hardware is managed by the hypervisor, which allocates the necessary resources from the host system to ensure that the VM operates correctly.

The emulation of virtual CPUs is one of the most critical aspects of hardware emulation in virtual machines. A virtual CPU (vCPU) acts as the central processing unit for the VM, allowing it to execute instructions and run software. The hypervisor allocates a portion of the host system's physical CPU to each vCPU, ensuring that the virtual machine can carry out processing tasks. Since a physical CPU is shared between multiple VMs, the hypervisor schedules CPU time for each vCPU, allowing it to run concurrently with other virtual machines and the host system. The virtual CPU is often designed to resemble a physical CPU, providing the VM with the same functionality that a physical machine would offer, albeit within a virtualized environment.

Virtual memory is another essential component of hardware emulation in virtual machines. Each virtual machine requires memory in order to store running processes, system files, and data. The hypervisor manages virtual memory by allocating physical memory from the host system to the virtual machines as needed. When the virtual machine runs out of memory, the hypervisor can employ techniques such as paging or memory ballooning to ensure that the VM receives additional resources. Memory virtualization allows virtual machines to operate as though they have dedicated memory, despite sharing physical memory with other VMs and the host system. This isolation is vital for ensuring that virtual machines do not interfere with one another, making it possible to run multiple operating systems concurrently on a single physical system.

In addition to virtual CPUs and memory, virtual storage is another key aspect of hardware emulation. Virtual machines use virtual disks, which are typically stored as files on the host system's physical storage.

These virtual disks are presented to the VM as physical hard drives, allowing the operating system within the virtual machine to interact with them in the same way it would with a physical disk. The hypervisor controls how data is read from and written to these virtual disks, mapping them to the host system's physical storage. Virtual disks can be configured to be dynamically allocated, meaning that the disk size will grow as data is written to it, or fixed in size, meaning that the disk will not grow beyond a set capacity. This flexibility allows for efficient storage management and ensures that virtual machines can scale based on their storage needs.

Virtual network adapters are another critical component of hardware emulation in virtual machines. Networking is essential for most virtual machines, as they often need to communicate with other VMs or external systems. The hypervisor provides virtual network interfaces to each VM, which can be configured to operate in different network modes, such as bridged, NAT (network address translation), or host-only networking. In a bridged network mode, the virtual machine is connected directly to the host's physical network interface, allowing it to communicate with other devices on the network as though it were a physical machine. In NAT mode, the virtual machine shares the host system's IP address, using network address translation to communicate with external networks. These virtual network adapters enable seamless communication between virtual machines and external resources, making it possible to run distributed applications or access the internet from within a virtualized environment.

The process of hardware emulation relies heavily on the hypervisor, which is responsible for managing the virtualized hardware and ensuring that each VM receives the appropriate resources. The hypervisor acts as an intermediary between the host system's physical hardware and the virtual machines, providing the necessary translation and management for the virtual hardware. There are two main types of hypervisors: Type 1 (bare-metal) and Type 2 (hosted). Type 1 hypervisors run directly on the host's physical hardware and provide direct access to the system's resources. In contrast, Type 2 hypervisors run on top of an existing operating system and rely on that OS to manage hardware resources. Both types of hypervisors handle hardware emulation in different ways, but the fundamental goal is the same: to provide virtual machines with a functional and isolated hardware environment.

While hardware emulation allows virtual machines to run software that requires specific hardware, it is important to note that there is always some level of overhead involved. The virtualized hardware is not as efficient as physical hardware because the hypervisor must translate requests between the virtual hardware and the physical system. This overhead can impact the performance of resource-intensive applications or high-performance computing tasks. However, modern hypervisors and hardware-assisted virtualization features, such as Intel VT-x and AMD-V, have significantly reduced this overhead, enabling virtual machines to operate at near-native performance levels. Despite these advances, there may still be cases where the performance of virtualized hardware falls short of that of dedicated physical hardware, particularly for applications that require direct access to hardware resources, such as gaming or high-performance computing.

Hardware emulation is also a key factor in the flexibility of virtual machines. The ability to run different operating systems on the same physical machine, each with its own set of virtualized hardware, opens up a wide range of possibilities for testing, development, and deployment. For instance, developers can create virtual environments that mimic specific hardware configurations, enabling them to test software in different scenarios without needing physical machines for each configuration. Similarly, virtual machines can be easily migrated between host systems, allowing for more efficient resource utilization and disaster recovery.

Overall, virtual machine hardware emulation enables the creation of flexible, efficient, and isolated virtualized environments that can mimic the functionality of physical systems. By abstracting the underlying hardware, virtualization allows for the efficient sharing of physical resources and makes it possible to run multiple operating systems on a single physical machine. The emulation of CPUs, memory, storage, and networking interfaces provides virtual machines with the necessary components to operate as fully functional systems, supporting a wide range of use cases from development and testing to cloud computing and data center virtualization. The ability to emulate hardware is what makes virtualization a powerful and versatile tool in modern IT infrastructure.

Resource Allocation in Virtual Machines

Resource allocation in virtual machines (VMs) is a fundamental concept that determines how computing resources such as CPU, memory, storage, and network bandwidth are distributed across virtualized environments. In a virtualized system, multiple VMs run concurrently on the same physical hardware, and it is the responsibility of the hypervisor to allocate resources in a way that ensures each VM operates efficiently and without interference from other VMs. Proper resource allocation is crucial for maintaining the performance, stability, and security of virtualized environments, particularly in scenarios involving resource-intensive applications or large-scale deployments. The ability to effectively allocate resources to virtual machines allows organizations to maximize the potential of their hardware and optimize their computing infrastructure.

One of the key elements of resource allocation in virtual machines is the management of CPU resources. The CPU is the most critical resource in any computing environment, and in virtualized systems, it is shared among multiple VMs. Each VM is allocated a certain number of virtual CPUs (vCPUs), which are essentially virtual representations of the host machine's physical CPU cores. The hypervisor is responsible for scheduling CPU time for each vCPU, ensuring that each VM receives an appropriate share of the host system's processing power. In some cases, the hypervisor uses techniques such as time-slicing to allocate CPU time to each VM in turn, while in other cases, it may use more sophisticated scheduling algorithms to allocate CPU resources based on the priority or workload demands of each VM.

The management of CPU resources becomes more complex in environments where multiple VMs are running demanding applications or high-performance workloads. In these cases, the hypervisor must ensure that CPU resources are distributed in such a way that performance is not compromised. Techniques such as CPU affinity and resource limits can be employed to ensure that critical VMs receive the necessary processing power, while less demanding VMs are allocated fewer CPU resources. CPU affinity refers to the practice of binding a particular VM to specific physical CPU cores, which can help optimize performance by reducing the overhead associated with CPU context switching. Resource limits, on the other hand, allow administrators to set upper limits on the amount of CPU time a VM can consume, preventing any single VM from monopolizing the host system's processing power.

Memory allocation in virtual machines is another critical aspect of resource management. In virtualized environments, each VM is allocated a certain amount of memory, which is managed by the hypervisor. This virtual memory is mapped to the host's physical memory, and the hypervisor is responsible for ensuring that each VM receives the required amount of memory to run its operating system and applications. Memory allocation can be static or dynamic, depending on the configuration of the virtual machine. Static memory allocation assigns a fixed amount of memory to a VM, ensuring that it always has access to the same amount of physical memory, regardless of its workload. Dynamic memory allocation, on the other hand, allows the hypervisor to adjust the amount of memory allocated to a VM based on its current demands. This flexibility is particularly useful in environments where workloads fluctuate, as it ensures that resources are utilized efficiently without wasting memory.

In larger virtualized environments, memory management can become more complex, particularly when multiple VMs are running on the same host system. Resource contention can arise when the total memory demand from all VMs exceeds the available physical memory on the host system. To manage this, hypervisors use techniques such as memory ballooning, swapping, and compression to allocate memory efficiently. Memory ballooning allows the hypervisor to reclaim memory from idle or low-priority VMs and allocate it to more resource-intensive VMs. Swapping involves moving pages of memory from the physical memory to disk storage when there is insufficient memory available, although this can result in slower performance. Memory compression is another technique that allows the hypervisor to compress memory pages to free up space and improve memory utilization.

Storage allocation is also an essential component of resource management in virtual machines. Each VM is assigned virtual disks, which are essentially files stored on the host system's physical storage. The hypervisor manages these virtual disks, ensuring that data is written to and read from the appropriate physical storage locations. Virtual disks can be configured to be either dynamically allocated or fixed in size. Dynamically allocated disks grow in size as data is added to them, while fixed-size disks occupy a set amount of physical storage from the outset. The hypervisor also manages storage I/O, ensuring that each VM has access to the necessary storage resources without causing bottlenecks or performance degradation. In large virtualized environments, shared storage systems, such as network-attached storage (NAS) or storage area networks (SAN), are often used to provide high-performance, centralized storage for VMs.

Network resource allocation is equally important in virtualized environments. Each virtual machine is typically provided with one or more virtual network adapters, which allow it to communicate with other VMs and external networks. The hypervisor manages network traffic between virtual machines and between VMs and the outside world. In most cases, the virtual network adapters of the VMs are connected to virtual switches, which are managed by the hypervisor and function similarly to physical network switches. These virtual switches allow VMs to communicate with each other and with external devices, such as routers and firewalls. In addition to providing connectivity, the hypervisor may also offer features such as network traffic isolation, security policies, and quality of service (QoS) to manage bandwidth and prevent network congestion.

In larger virtualized environments, managing network resources effectively is critical for maintaining performance and ensuring that VMs can communicate without delay. Hypervisors often support advanced networking features such as VLANs (virtual local area networks), which allow VMs to be grouped into isolated networks, and network traffic shaping, which enables administrators to control the flow of data to prevent congestion. These features help ensure that network resources are allocated efficiently and that VMs are able to communicate with minimal latency.

Effective resource allocation in virtual machines also requires monitoring and management tools to ensure that resources are being used optimally. Many hypervisors come with built-in monitoring tools that allow administrators to track resource usage across multiple VMs. These tools provide insights into CPU, memory, storage, and network utilization, helping administrators identify potential performance issues or resource bottlenecks. In addition to monitoring, resource scheduling and load balancing are also essential for ensuring that virtual machines receive the necessary resources to operate efficiently. Load balancing algorithms can be used to distribute workloads across multiple physical hosts, preventing any single host from becoming overloaded and ensuring that resources are allocated dynamically based on demand.

Resource allocation in virtual machines is a critical aspect of virtualization that directly impacts the performance and efficiency of virtualized environments. Properly managing CPU, memory, storage, and network resources ensures that each VM operates optimally without interfering with other VMs on the same host. As virtualized environments continue to grow in size and complexity, efficient resource allocation becomes even more important for maintaining performance, scalability, and cost-effectiveness. By using advanced techniques such as dynamic memory allocation, resource scheduling, and load balancing, hypervisors can ensure that virtualized environments operate smoothly, even under heavy workloads. Effective resource management is essential for maximizing the benefits of virtualization and supporting the demands of modern IT infrastructures.

Virtual CPUs: Allocation and Management

Virtual CPUs (vCPUs) are a fundamental component of virtualized environments, providing the processing power required to run virtual machines (VMs). In a virtualized system, multiple VMs can share the physical resources of a single host system, including its central processing unit (CPU). Each VM is allocated one or more vCPUs, which act as virtual representations of the physical CPU cores on the host machine. The hypervisor, responsible for managing the virtualized environment, is tasked with efficiently allocating CPU resources to the VMs while ensuring that each VM has sufficient processing power to perform its tasks. The allocation and management of vCPUs are crucial to maintaining the performance, efficiency, and stability of virtualized systems.

When a virtual machine is created, the hypervisor allocates vCPUs to the VM based on its requirements and the available physical CPU resources on the host system. The number of vCPUs assigned to a VM depends on several factors, including the workload it is expected to handle, the number of physical CPU cores available, and the performance demands of the applications running within the VM. The hypervisor ensures that the total number of vCPUs across all VMs does not exceed the number of physical CPU cores available on the host, although in many cases, vCPUs can be overcommitted, allowing multiple virtual CPUs to share a physical CPU core. This approach is often used to maximize the utilization of the host's resources, particularly in environments where the VMs do not require constant access to the full processing power of the CPU.

The allocation of vCPUs is not a one-time process but an ongoing task that requires continuous management. As workloads and resource demands fluctuate, the hypervisor may need to adjust the allocation of vCPUs to ensure that each VM receives the appropriate level of processing power. This dynamic allocation is particularly important in environments where workloads are highly variable, such as cloud platforms or data centers, where the number of active VMs can change frequently. Hypervisors typically provide features such as resource scheduling and dynamic resource allocation, which allow the system to adapt to changing demands and ensure that VMs continue to run smoothly, even under varying levels of load.

One key concept in the management of vCPUs is the idea of CPU scheduling. Since multiple VMs may be running on the same physical host, the hypervisor is responsible for scheduling the execution of their vCPUs on the physical CPU cores. This scheduling process ensures that each VM receives a fair share of the CPU resources and that the overall performance of the system is maintained. CPU scheduling in virtualized environments can be more complex than in physical systems, as it must account for the fact that VMs are sharing the same physical hardware. The hypervisor uses various scheduling algorithms to allocate CPU time to each vCPU, taking into account factors such as the priority of the VM, the current CPU load, and the number of vCPUs assigned to each VM. Some hypervisors also offer features like CPU affinity, which allows the administrator to bind specific vCPUs to particular physical CPU cores. This can help optimize performance in situations where certain VMs need dedicated processing power for resource-intensive tasks.

Another important aspect of vCPU allocation is CPU overcommitment. In virtualized environments, it is common to allocate more vCPUs to VMs than the number of physical CPU cores available on the host system. This approach, known as CPU overcommitment, allows for more efficient utilization of CPU resources, particularly in scenarios where VMs do not constantly require full access to CPU power. While overcommitting CPUs can lead to better resource utilization, it also introduces the risk of resource contention, where multiple VMs compete for limited CPU resources, potentially leading to performance degradation. The hypervisor must carefully manage overcommitment by using techniques like time-slicing, which allocates CPU time in small intervals to each vCPU, ensuring that all VMs receive a fair share of processing power. In some cases, administrators may need to adjust the number of vCPUs assigned to each VM or reduce overcommitment to prevent performance bottlenecks.

The performance of vCPUs is influenced by several factors, including the number of physical CPU cores, the architecture of the host system's CPU, and the workload of the VMs. Virtual machines with more vCPUs can often handle more demanding workloads, but allocating too many vCPUs can lead to inefficient use of resources, especially if the VM does not require that level of processing power. Conversely, allocating too few vCPUs to a VM can result in poor performance, particularly for resource-intensive applications. Hypervisors typically provide tools for monitoring and optimizing vCPU performance, allowing administrators to track CPU usage, identify bottlenecks, and adjust the allocation of vCPUs as needed. These tools may include real-time performance metrics, alerts for resource contention, and automated recommendations for resource allocation.

In cloud computing environments, the allocation and management of vCPUs are particularly important for ensuring efficient resource utilization and cost management. Cloud providers often rely on virtualization to deliver Infrastructure as a Service (IaaS) to customers, allowing them to provision and manage VMs on-demand. The ability to allocate vCPUs dynamically and efficiently is key to providing flexible, scalable, and cost-effective services. Cloud providers typically offer customers the option to select the number of vCPUs they require when provisioning a VM, with the cost of the service often tied to the number of vCPUs allocated. By effectively managing vCPU allocation, cloud providers can ensure that resources are used efficiently, minimizing wasted capacity and maximizing the performance of their infrastructure.

The management of vCPUs also plays a crucial role in ensuring the security and isolation of virtualized environments. Because vCPUs are virtualized representations of physical CPUs, they must be carefully isolated from one another to prevent interference or unauthorized access. Hypervisors provide mechanisms for securing vCPU allocation, ensuring that each VM's vCPUs are isolated from those of other VMs. In multi-tenant environments, where multiple organizations may be running their VMs on the same physical hardware, this isolation is particularly important for preventing cross-VM attacks or unauthorized access to sensitive data. The hypervisor ensures that vCPUs cannot directly access the memory or resources of other VMs, providing a secure environment for running applications and workloads.

The management of virtual CPUs is a critical aspect of resource allocation in virtualized systems. By allocating and managing vCPUs efficiently, the hypervisor ensures that each virtual machine receives the necessary processing power to operate effectively. This management includes tasks such as CPU scheduling, overcommitment, performance monitoring, and resource isolation, all of which are essential for maintaining the performance, security, and stability of virtualized environments. Whether in a data center, cloud platform, or desktop virtualization setup, the effective management of vCPUs is key to optimizing resource usage and delivering reliable, high-performance virtualized systems. The ability to allocate and manage vCPUs efficiently is fundamental to the success of virtualization technology and plays a central role in the broader ecosystem of modern IT infrastructure.

Memory Management in Virtual Machines

Memory management is a crucial aspect of virtualization, as it determines how memory is allocated, used, and optimized in virtual machines (VMs). In a physical system, memory is allocated directly from the host system's physical memory to the operating system and applications. However, in virtualized environments, where multiple VMs share the same physical host, memory management becomes more complex. The hypervisor, which controls the virtualized environment, is responsible for efficiently allocating memory to each VM, ensuring that the virtual machines can run their operating systems and applications effectively without exceeding the available physical resources.

At the core of memory management in virtual machines is the concept of virtual memory. Each virtual machine is allocated a certain amount of virtual memory, which appears to the guest operating system as if it were a dedicated resource. This virtual memory is mapped to the physical memory of the host system by the hypervisor, ensuring that the VM operates as though it has its own independent memory space. The hypervisor manages this mapping, translating memory requests from the VM into physical memory accesses on the host system. This abstraction allows for more efficient resource utilization, as the physical memory of the host can be shared across multiple virtual machines.

One of the primary challenges of memory management in virtual machines is ensuring that the available physical memory is allocated efficiently across all running VMs. Memory allocation in a virtualized environment is not a static process; rather, it must be dynamic to adapt to the changing needs of the VMs. When a VM is first created, it is allocated a fixed amount of memory, which is typically set based on the expected workload. However, as the VM runs, its memory requirements may change. The hypervisor must monitor the memory usage of each VM in real time and adjust the allocation as needed. This dynamic allocation ensures that each VM receives the necessary resources to perform its tasks, while also preventing any one VM from consuming all of the host's memory and causing resource contention.

In some cases, memory overcommitment can be used to allocate more virtual memory to VMs than the physical memory available on the host system. This technique is possible because not all VMs require their full allocation of memory at all times. For example, if a VM is idle or running low-intensity tasks, it may not need the full amount of memory allocated to it. The hypervisor can take advantage of this by overcommitting memory, allowing multiple VMs to share the available physical memory. However, memory overcommitment introduces the risk of performance degradation, as the hypervisor must employ techniques such as paging or swapping to ensure that memory requests are met. These techniques can lead to slower performance if the system is unable to allocate memory quickly enough, particularly in environments with high memory demands.

To manage memory more efficiently, modern hypervisors implement several advanced memory management techniques. One such technique is memory ballooning, which allows the hypervisor to dynamically adjust the memory allocated to each VM based on its current needs. In a ballooning scenario, the hypervisor uses a special balloon driver installed within the guest operating system to reclaim unused memory from the VM. The balloon driver inflates when the system needs more memory and deflates when the VM requires less. This technique enables the hypervisor to redistribute memory across VMs, freeing up resources from idle VMs and allocating them to more active ones. Memory ballooning helps ensure that memory is utilized more efficiently, especially in environments where workloads fluctuate.

Another important technique in memory management is memory deduplication, which aims to reduce the amount of duplicated memory between VMs. In virtualized environments, multiple VMs may run similar operating systems or applications that share common files and libraries. Memory deduplication identifies these shared components and eliminates the redundancy by storing only one copy in the host's physical memory. This allows the hypervisor to reclaim memory that would otherwise be wasted on duplicated data, increasing the overall memory efficiency of the system. Deduplication is particularly effective in environments where multiple VMs are running similar workloads, such as in cloud data centers or testing environments.

Swapping and paging are other techniques used by hypervisors to manage memory in virtualized environments. When a VM's memory demand exceeds the available physical memory on the host, the hypervisor can swap out less frequently used pages of memory to disk storage, freeing up physical memory for more active processes. While swapping can help prevent a VM from running out of memory, it can also lead to slower performance, as disk access is much slower than accessing memory. Hypervisors can also use paging, which involves moving smaller chunks of memory, known as pages, between the physical memory and storage. Although paging allows for more fine-grained control over memory allocation, it also introduces additional overhead and can impact performance if used excessively.

In addition to these memory management techniques, modern hypervisors provide tools to monitor and optimize memory usage in virtualized environments. Administrators can track the memory consumption of individual VMs, identify potential memory bottlenecks, and take corrective action when necessary. For example, if a VM is consistently consuming more memory than it has been allocated, the administrator can adjust the memory allocation or investigate the workload to determine if there are memory leaks or inefficient processes running. Hypervisors also provide tools for setting memory limits and priorities, which allow administrators to control how memory is distributed among VMs. By setting limits, administrators can prevent a single VM from consuming excessive memory and affecting the performance of other VMs running on the same host.

The ability to efficiently manage memory in virtual machines is critical for ensuring the overall performance and stability of virtualized environments. As the number of VMs increases, memory management becomes even more complex, requiring advanced techniques to ensure that each VM has access to the necessary resources while preventing contention between VMs. The hypervisor must constantly monitor memory usage, allocate resources dynamically, and employ techniques such as ballooning, deduplication, and swapping to optimize memory utilization. In cloud computing environments or large-scale data centers, where hundreds or even thousands of VMs may be running on the same physical hardware, effective memory management is essential for maximizing the efficiency of the infrastructure and ensuring that workloads run smoothly.

Furthermore, memory management plays a key role in ensuring the security and isolation of virtualized environments. Because multiple VMs share the same physical memory, the hypervisor must ensure that the memory of one VM is protected from unauthorized access by other VMs. Memory isolation is crucial in multi-tenant environments, where different organizations or users may be running their VMs on the same host. The hypervisor enforces memory isolation to prevent one VM from accessing the memory of another, protecting sensitive data and preventing potential security breaches. This isolation ensures that each VM operates as though it has its own dedicated memory, even though the physical memory is shared.

Efficient memory management in virtual machines is essential for maintaining the performance, scalability, and security of virtualized environments. By utilizing advanced techniques such as ballooning, deduplication, swapping, and dynamic memory allocation, the hypervisor can ensure that memory resources are distributed optimally across all running VMs. These techniques allow virtualized environments to scale more effectively, ensuring that VMs have access to the necessary memory resources while minimizing the risk of performance degradation and resource contention. As the demand for virtualized systems continues to grow, memory management will remain a critical factor in ensuring the success of virtualization technology.

Disk Storage Options for Virtual Machines

Disk storage is an essential component of virtualized environments, as virtual machines (VMs) rely on disk storage to store their operating systems, applications, and data. In virtualized environments, the way disk storage is managed and allocated differs from traditional physical systems. Disk storage for virtual machines is typically abstracted from the underlying physical hardware, allowing multiple VMs to share the same physical storage resources. The hypervisor, which manages the virtualized environment, is responsible for allocating storage to each VM, ensuring that each one has the necessary resources to function effectively. Understanding the different disk storage options available for virtual machines is crucial for optimizing performance, scalability, and resource utilization in virtualized systems.

One of the most common disk storage options for virtual machines is the use of virtual disks. A virtual disk is a file that resides on the host system's physical storage and acts as the storage medium for the VM. Virtual disks are managed by the hypervisor and are presented to the virtual machine as if they were physical hard drives. Each VM can have one or more virtual disks, and these virtual disks function just like physical disks within the guest operating system. The hypervisor handles the mapping of the virtual disks to the host's physical storage, ensuring that data is read from and written to the correct location on the physical disk.

There are several types of virtual disks, each with its own characteristics and use cases. One of the most common types is the dynamically allocated virtual disk. With dynamically allocated disks, the virtual disk starts with a small size and grows as data is added to it. This allows for efficient use of storage, as the disk only consumes as much space as is necessary to store the data. Dynamically allocated disks are often used when the storage requirements of a virtual machine are not known in advance, or when the storage needs fluctuate over time. This type of disk provides flexibility and ensures that storage is not wasted, as it grows in size only when needed.

Another common type of virtual disk is the fixed-size disk. Fixed-size disks are allocated a specific amount of storage when the virtual disk is created. The disk size does not change, even if the VM does not use all of the allocated space. Fixed-size disks offer better performance than dynamically allocated disks, as there is no overhead associated with resizing the disk as data is added. However, fixed-size disks can lead to inefficient use of storage, particularly if the virtual machine does not use the entire allocated space. They are often used in environments where performance is a priority, and the storage requirements of the VM are well known in advance.

Thin provisioning is another disk storage option commonly used in virtualized environments. Thin provisioning allows administrators to allocate more storage to virtual machines than is physically available on the host system. With thin provisioning, virtual disks are created with a large capacity, but the physical storage is only used as data is written to the disk. This allows for more efficient utilization of storage resources, as VMs can be allocated more storage than is physically available, with the hypervisor ensuring that storage is not overcommitted. However, thin provisioning requires careful monitoring to ensure that the host system does not run out of physical storage, as VMs may exceed the physical capacity of the storage system if their disk usage grows faster than expected.

In addition to virtual disks, virtualized environments often use shared storage to provide centralized storage for multiple virtual machines. Shared storage allows multiple VMs to access the same storage resources, making it ideal for environments where VMs need to share data or where high availability and fault tolerance are required. Shared storage systems, such as network-attached storage (NAS) or storage area networks (SAN), are commonly used in enterprise-level virtualized environments and cloud computing platforms. Shared storage enables features such as VM migration, where a virtual machine can be moved from one host to another without downtime. This is possible because the virtual machine's storage is separate from the host's local storage and can be accessed from any host connected to the shared storage system.

One of the primary benefits of using shared storage is the ability to implement high availability and disaster recovery solutions. In a virtualized environment, shared storage allows virtual machines to be replicated or backed up to a remote location, ensuring that critical data is protected in the event of hardware failure or disaster. Additionally, shared storage allows for the use of advanced storage techniques, such as deduplication, where redundant data is eliminated, and only unique data is stored. This can significantly reduce storage requirements and improve the efficiency of virtualized systems.

A key consideration when using shared storage in virtualized environments is performance. Shared storage systems, particularly those that rely on network connections, can introduce latency or bottlenecks if the network infrastructure is not properly configured. High-performance shared storage systems, such as all-flash arrays, are often used to minimize latency and provide fast access to storage for virtual machines. These systems can be particularly beneficial in environments where I/O performance is critical, such as in databases or high-performance computing applications. However, shared storage systems can be more expensive than local storage, making them more suitable for larger-scale deployments or environments where performance and availability are top priorities.

Local storage, on the other hand, is another option for disk storage in virtual machines. Local storage refers to storage that is directly attached to the host machine, such as hard drives or solid-state drives (SSDs) that are physically installed on the host system. Virtual machines can be allocated local storage for their virtual disks, which can provide high performance and low latency, particularly if the host system is equipped with fast storage devices like SSDs. Local storage is typically used in small-scale virtualized environments or in cases where high-performance storage is required for specific VMs. However, local storage has limitations in terms of scalability and redundancy. If a host machine fails, any data stored on its local drives may be lost, unless additional measures, such as replication or backup, are implemented.

Disk storage options for virtual machines also include the ability to use virtualized storage technologies, such as virtual storage area networks (vSANs). A vSAN is a software-defined storage solution that aggregates local storage from multiple physical hosts to create a shared storage pool. vSANs provide the benefits of shared storage, such as centralized management and high availability, but without the need for dedicated external storage devices. vSANs are often used in hyper-converged infrastructures, where compute and storage resources are integrated into a single platform. This type of storage solution is particularly effective for scaling storage in virtualized environments and provides a cost-effective alternative to traditional shared storage systems.

Disk storage is a critical element in virtualized environments, and selecting the appropriate storage solution is essential for optimizing performance, efficiency, and scalability. Virtual disks, shared storage, and local storage each have their own advantages and trade-offs, and the choice of storage option will depend on factors such as the specific workload, performance requirements, and budget. By understanding the different disk storage options available, administrators can design virtualized systems that meet the needs of their organizations while maximizing the benefits of virtualization technology. Whether using local disks, shared storage systems, or advanced software-defined storage solutions, the effective management of disk storage is key to the success of virtualized environments.

Network Configuration in Virtualized Environments

In virtualized environments, network configuration plays a critical role in ensuring the proper operation and performance of virtual machines (VMs). As virtualized environments allow for the creation and management of multiple VMs running on a single physical host, it becomes essential to design and configure the network to ensure seamless communication between the VMs, the host system, and external networks. Unlike traditional physical machines, which have direct access to network interfaces, virtualized systems must rely on the hypervisor to manage network connections and resources. The network configuration in such environments is designed to provide isolation, performance, and security while allowing flexibility and scalability.

In a virtualized environment, each virtual machine is typically assigned a virtual network adapter. This virtual adapter is similar to a physical network interface card (NIC) but exists solely within the virtualized environment. The virtual adapter allows the VM to send and receive data as if it were a physical machine, even though the network traffic is being handled by the host system. The hypervisor plays a central role in managing the virtual network adapters, ensuring that each VM is connected to the appropriate network and that network traffic is routed efficiently.

One of the primary components of network configuration in virtualized environments is the virtual switch. A virtual switch is a software-based network switch that operates within the hypervisor to connect virtual machines to each other and to external networks. The virtual switch functions similarly to a physical network switch by forwarding network packets between virtual machines or between a virtual machine and the host system. Virtual switches are capable of supporting multiple network configurations, including bridging, network address translation (NAT), and host-only networking. The choice of configuration depends on the desired level of isolation and communication between the virtual machines and external resources.

Bridged networking is one of the most common network configurations in virtualized environments. In a bridged network setup, the virtual switch connects the virtual machines directly to the physical network interface of the host system. This allows the virtual machines to be part of the same network as the host and communicate with other devices on the network as if they were physical machines. The virtual machines receive IP addresses from the same network DHCP server as the host, and they are accessible from other devices on the network. Bridged networking is ideal for environments where VMs need to interact with external systems, such as in testing, development, or production environments where VMs must communicate with other servers, workstations, or services.

Network Address Translation (NAT) is another popular network configuration in virtualized environments. With NAT, the virtual machines are connected to the host system through a virtual switch, but instead of receiving IP addresses from the physical network, they are assigned private IP addresses. The host system acts as a gateway, translating the private IP addresses of the virtual machines into the public IP address of the host system. This allows the virtual machines to access external networks, such as the internet, without exposing them directly to external devices. NAT is commonly used when there is a need to isolate the virtual machines from the external network for security or resource management reasons, while still allowing them to access external resources like web servers or databases.

Host-only networking is another type of network configuration used in virtualized environments. In a host-only network, the virtual machines are connected to a virtual switch that is isolated from the physical network. The virtual machines can communicate with each other and with the host system, but they cannot access external networks. This type of configuration is often used for testing or development environments where external network access is not necessary, and isolation between the virtual machines and the external world is desired. Host-only networking provides a secure, controlled environment for testing applications, running simulations, or troubleshooting issues without the risk of affecting external systems.

In addition to these basic networking configurations, more advanced network features are often required in large-scale virtualized environments, such as those found in data centers or cloud computing platforms. Virtualized network environments often require additional layers of security, performance optimization, and redundancy to ensure that the virtual machines remain secure, perform efficiently, and are highly available. Virtual local area networks (VLANs) are commonly used in such environments to segment network traffic and provide isolation between different types of network traffic or groups of virtual machines. By grouping virtual machines into separate VLANs, administrators can control the flow of traffic, ensuring that sensitive data is kept isolated from less secure network segments. VLANs also help in optimizing network traffic by reducing broadcast domains, improving performance and network efficiency.

Software-defined networking (SDN) is another advanced network configuration used in modern virtualized environments. SDN allows for the centralization of network control and management by decoupling the control plane from the data plane. In traditional network configurations, the control and data planes are tightly coupled, meaning that the network devices make decisions about how data is forwarded. In an SDN environment, the control plane is centralized in a software controller, which manages and directs network traffic across the entire infrastructure. This enables more flexible and dynamic network configurations, allowing administrators to easily adjust network settings, optimize traffic flows, and implement security policies without needing to make changes at the hardware level. SDN is particularly useful in large-scale environments where the network configuration must be highly flexible and responsive to changing demands.

Virtual network adapters and virtual switches are not only responsible for connecting virtual machines to one another but also for ensuring that network traffic is secure. Network security in virtualized environments requires careful management of virtual networks to prevent unauthorized access and ensure that sensitive data remains protected. Hypervisors typically provide security features such as virtual firewalls, network isolation, and traffic filtering to secure the virtual machines and their communication channels. Virtual firewalls can be used to protect virtual machines from external attacks or unauthorized access, while network isolation ensures that certain VMs are unable to communicate with others unless explicitly allowed. Traffic filtering can be implemented to restrict certain types of network traffic, further enhancing the security of the virtualized network.

Another critical aspect of network configuration in virtualized environments is network performance optimization. The performance of virtualized networks can be affected by several factors, including the number of virtual machines running on a single host, the type of network traffic being generated, and the bandwidth available on the physical network. Hypervisors typically offer network performance tuning features that allow administrators to optimize the flow of data between virtual machines and external networks. These features may include quality of service (QoS) settings, which prioritize certain types of traffic, or the ability to adjust network adapter settings to improve throughput and reduce latency. Optimizing network performance ensures that virtual machines can communicate efficiently without experiencing delays or disruptions.

The network configuration in virtualized environments must balance several factors, including performance, security, scalability, and isolation. The flexibility of virtualized networks allows for the implementation of various configurations, from basic setups like bridged or NAT networking to more advanced solutions such as SDN or VLANs. The choice of configuration depends on the specific needs of the virtualized environment, whether it is for testing, development, production, or large-scale cloud deployments. By carefully managing the virtualized network infrastructure, administrators can ensure that the virtual machines are able to communicate effectively and securely, while also optimizing performance and scalability for future growth. Network configuration in virtualized environments is not just about connecting virtual machines but about providing the necessary foundation for a robust, high-performing, and secure IT infrastructure.

Snapshot Technology: Concepts and Benefits

Snapshot technology is a vital tool in virtualized environments, providing a powerful mechanism for capturing the state of a virtual machine (VM) at a specific point in time. A snapshot is essentially a read-only copy of a VM's state, including its disk contents, memory, and configuration settings. By taking a snapshot, administrators can preserve the exact configuration of a VM, including its operating system, applications, and data, which can later be restored if necessary. Snapshots enable greater flexibility and efficiency in managing virtualized systems by offering a way to quickly revert to a previous working state, facilitating tasks such as testing, troubleshooting, and disaster recovery.

The fundamental concept behind snapshots is that they capture the exact state of a virtual machine at the time the snapshot is taken. This includes not only the disk contents, but also the memory state of the VM. When a snapshot is created, the hypervisor creates a new file that represents the point-in-time copy of the VM. As changes are made to the VM, they are written to new disk blocks, leaving the original snapshot intact. This technique allows for the preservation of the VM's state while allowing it to continue operating normally. When the snapshot is reverted, the VM is restored to the exact state it was in when the snapshot was taken, including its data, memory, and system settings.

One of the primary benefits of snapshot technology is the ability to perform safe and efficient system testing. When testing new software, configurations, or updates, it is often necessary to create a controlled environment in which changes can be made without the risk of negatively affecting the system. Snapshots provide a way to capture the state of a VM before any changes are made, allowing administrators to quickly revert to the original state if something goes wrong. This is particularly useful in development and testing environments, where software and configurations are frequently changed and tested. By using snapshots, developers and testers can ensure that any changes can be undone with minimal downtime, avoiding the need to reinstall or reconfigure the system from scratch.

Snapshots also play a crucial role in system troubleshooting and recovery. When an issue arises in a virtual machine, it may be necessary to diagnose and resolve the problem without causing further damage or loss of data. Snapshots allow administrators to quickly restore the VM to a known, stable state, enabling them to isolate and address the issue. For example, if a software update causes an application to crash or a configuration change results in system instability, administrators can revert to a previous snapshot to restore functionality. This ability to quickly restore a VM to a previous state minimizes downtime and reduces the risk of data loss, making snapshots an invaluable tool for maintaining system stability and reliability.

In addition to testing and troubleshooting, snapshots are essential for disaster recovery in virtualized environments. In the event of a system failure, such as hardware failure, power loss, or corruption of data, snapshots provide a way to recover the VM to its last known good state. By maintaining a regular schedule of snapshots, administrators can ensure that they have a backup of the VM at various stages, which can be used for recovery in case of an emergency. Snapshots can be taken before significant changes, such as software updates, configuration changes, or major application deployments, ensuring that administrators have a recovery point if anything goes wrong. This provides an additional layer of protection for virtual machines and the data they contain, enabling organizations to recover more quickly from unexpected events and minimize the impact of downtime.

Another important advantage of snapshot technology is its ability to facilitate VM migration and cloning. Snapshots can be used to create a copy of a virtual machine that can be deployed to another host or location. This is particularly useful in cloud computing environments, where virtual machines need to be moved between different physical hosts or data centers. By creating a snapshot of a VM, administrators can ensure that the VM is in a consistent state before it is migrated, reducing the risk of data corruption or configuration errors during the migration process. Snapshots can also be used to create VM templates, which are pre-configured virtual machines that can be cloned and deployed quickly to meet changing workload demands. This enables organizations to scale their virtualized environments more efficiently and respond to changing resource requirements with minimal effort.

Despite the numerous benefits of snapshot technology, there are also some limitations and considerations that administrators must be aware of. One of the main challenges associated with snapshots is the potential impact on disk space. As snapshots capture the entire state of the virtual machine, including its disk contents, multiple snapshots can quickly consume significant amounts of storage. This can be particularly problematic in environments where many snapshots are created and retained over time. To mitigate this, administrators must carefully manage snapshots, ensuring that they are deleted when no longer needed to free up storage space. It is also important to note that excessive use of snapshots can degrade performance, as the hypervisor must track changes made to the virtual machine after the snapshot is taken. This can lead to increased overhead and slower disk I/O performance, particularly when the VM is running resource-intensive workloads.

Another limitation of snapshots is that they are typically designed for short-term use. While snapshots are ideal for testing, troubleshooting, and recovery, they are not meant to be used as a long-term backup solution. Over time, the complexity of managing multiple snapshots can increase, and the performance impact of maintaining snapshots may become more noticeable. For long-term backups, administrators should consider using dedicated backup solutions that are specifically designed for VM backup and restoration. These solutions typically offer more robust features, such as incremental backups, compression, and off-site storage, which can help address the limitations of snapshots in terms of long-term storage and performance.

In some cases, the use of snapshots in production environments can be risky if not properly managed. For example, if a snapshot is taken and then not properly deleted or maintained, it can lead to storage and performance issues that affect the overall health of the virtualized environment. Administrators must ensure that snapshots are regularly cleaned up and that only the necessary snapshots are kept to avoid the accumulation of unnecessary data. Proper snapshot management practices, such as setting expiration dates for snapshots and automating the cleanup process, can help mitigate these risks and ensure that snapshots are used effectively without causing adverse effects on system performance or storage.

Snapshot technology is a powerful tool in virtualized environments, offering numerous benefits in terms of testing, troubleshooting, recovery, and scalability. The ability to capture and revert to a specific point in time allows administrators to manage virtual machines more efficiently, minimizing downtime and reducing the risk of data loss. While snapshots are not without their limitations, such as potential storage consumption and performance impact, they remain a critical part of modern virtualization management. By understanding the concepts and benefits of snapshot technology, administrators can leverage its capabilities to enhance the reliability and flexibility of their virtualized systems.

Creating and Managing Virtual Machine Snapshots

Creating and managing virtual machine (VM) snapshots is a crucial aspect of virtualization management, providing a powerful method for preserving the state of a virtual machine at a specific point in time. Snapshots allow system administrators to save a consistent image of a VM, including its operating system, applications, and configuration, which can later be reverted to in the event of a problem or during testing. This functionality greatly enhances the flexibility of virtualized environments, enabling quick recovery, experimentation, and easy rollback to known good configurations. However, effective management of snapshots requires a clear understanding of how they work, the potential impact on system performance, and best practices for maintaining a healthy virtual environment.

To begin with, creating a snapshot involves capturing the entire state of a virtual machine, including the virtual machine's disk state, memory, and configuration. When a snapshot is taken, the hypervisor creates a read-only copy of the VM's disk, and any subsequent changes to the VM are written to a new delta file. This process preserves the original state, allowing administrators to revert to it if needed. The snapshot also captures the VM's memory, so the state of running processes is preserved. When the VM is restored from a snapshot, it is returned to the exact state it was in when the snapshot was taken, including both the file system and the active memory content.

The ability to create a snapshot is particularly useful when administrators need to make changes to the virtual machine, such as applying software updates, configuring new settings, or installing applications. By creating a snapshot before making these changes, administrators can easily revert to the previous state if the changes cause unexpected issues or failures. This capability is invaluable in testing environments, where multiple configurations need to be tested, and the VM must be restored to a known state after each test iteration. Without snapshots, testing would be a much more tedious and error-prone process, often requiring manual reconfiguration or reinstallations.

When it comes to creating snapshots, there are a few considerations that must be taken into account. First, while snapshots are incredibly useful, they should not be overused. Each snapshot takes up additional storage space, as it records the state of the VM at the time it was created. As changes are made to the VM, the delta file grows in size, which can quickly consume storage space if snapshots are retained for long periods. It is crucial for administrators to implement a process for regularly reviewing and deleting outdated snapshots to free up storage and avoid unnecessary performance degradation. Additionally, snapshots are typically designed for short-term use and are not intended to serve as permanent backups. For long-term data protection, administrators should use dedicated backup solutions that are optimized for virtualized environments.

In terms of managing snapshots, one of the key tasks is determining when and how often to create them. Snapshots should be taken before performing any potentially disruptive changes, such as installing updates, applying patches, or changing system configurations. These snapshots allow for an easy rollback if the changes cause instability or system failures. It is also advisable to take snapshots before performing complex tasks that might introduce unexpected results, such as testing new applications or upgrading the operating system. By creating a snapshot before such activities, administrators can ensure that they have a safety net to return to if the environment becomes unstable.

Another important aspect of snapshot management is maintaining the integrity of the virtual machine's performance. While snapshots are an invaluable tool, they can impact system performance, especially when multiple snapshots are retained over time. When a snapshot is created, the virtual machine's disk is frozen in its current state, and any changes are written to a delta file. Over time, as more snapshots are created, these delta files can grow large, and the virtual machine's performance can degrade, as the hypervisor must track and manage changes to the original disk and its associated delta files. The more snapshots there are, the more resources the hypervisor must allocate to managing them, potentially slowing down the VM's performance.

To mitigate the performance impact of snapshots, it is essential to delete or consolidate snapshots when they are no longer needed. Many hypervisors provide tools for automatically merging or consolidating snapshots, which helps streamline the virtual machine's disk and restore the system to a single, consolidated state. This process merges the changes recorded in the delta files back into the original virtual disk, reducing the number of active snapshot files and improving performance. However, this process should be managed carefully, as consolidating snapshots can take time and could temporarily impact the performance of the virtual machine, especially if the VM is running high-demand applications.

Snapshot management also requires careful attention to the storage capacity of the virtualized environment. As snapshots grow in size, they can quickly consume available disk space, especially if the host system has limited storage resources. Administrators must ensure that adequate storage is available to accommodate the snapshot files, particularly in environments where many snapshots are created. It is also essential to set up automated alerts to notify administrators when the available storage is running low, allowing them to take action before the system runs into storage constraints. In large-scale virtualized environments, it is advisable to implement a storage management solution that can efficiently handle large volumes of snapshot data and provide adequate performance for the VMs.

In addition to storage management, administrators should consider the implications of snapshot usage on virtual machine replication and migration. In certain scenarios, VMs that are replicated or migrated from one host to another may encounter issues if snapshots are not handled correctly. For example, a VM with an active snapshot may experience inconsistencies when replicated or migrated, as the snapshot captures the state of the disk and memory, which may not be compatible with the new host system. To avoid such issues, it is best practice to delete or consolidate snapshots before migrating or replicating virtual machines. This ensures that the virtual machine's disk state is consistent and that the migration or replication process proceeds without errors.

When managing snapshots, administrators must also be mindful of the impact on backup strategies. While snapshots can be an effective way to protect a VM in the short term, they are not a substitute for a comprehensive backup plan. Snapshots are meant to capture a point-in-time image of the VM but do not offer the same level of protection as full backups, which are typically stored off-site or on dedicated backup systems. To ensure long-term data protection and availability, snapshots should be used in conjunction with regular backup strategies that include incremental or full backups, allowing administrators to recover data in the event of a disaster or hardware failure.

Creating and managing snapshots effectively requires a combination of careful planning, ongoing maintenance, and a clear understanding of the risks and limitations associated with snapshots. By using snapshots in conjunction with other backup and recovery strategies, administrators can enhance the resilience and flexibility of their virtualized environments, ensuring that virtual machines remain stable, secure, and efficient. The ability to revert to a previous snapshot provides a powerful safety net for virtualized systems, but it is important to follow best practices for snapshot management to avoid unnecessary performance degradation and storage issues. Properly managed, snapshots are an indispensable tool in maintaining the integrity of virtualized environments and ensuring business continuity.

Restoring Virtual Machines from Snapshots

Restoring virtual machines (VMs) from snapshots is a powerful and essential capability in virtualized environments. It allows system administrators to revert to a previously saved state of a VM, effectively undoing any changes made since the snapshot was created. This process provides flexibility and control in managing virtual machines, especially in situations where unforeseen issues arise, such as system failures, application errors, or configuration problems. Snapshots capture the exact state of a VM at a specific point in time, including its disk contents, memory, and configuration, allowing the restoration process to bring the VM back to its original condition. The ability to restore VMs from snapshots is invaluable for maintaining system stability, ensuring business continuity, and enhancing the efficiency of troubleshooting and testing.

The process of restoring a virtual machine from a snapshot typically begins when an issue arises that necessitates returning the VM to its previous state. For example, if a software update causes instability, or if an application installation leads to system crashes, administrators can restore the VM to a snapshot taken before the changes were made. This allows the VM to function normally again, without the need to manually undo or fix the changes. Restoring from a snapshot can be completed quickly and efficiently, often with minimal downtime. The snapshot's point-in-time nature means that both the VM's operating system and any applications running on it are returned to the exact state they were in at the moment the snapshot was taken, including the memory and any changes made to disk.

One of the key benefits of restoring virtual machines from snapshots is that it minimizes downtime. In a traditional physical system, restoring an operating system or recovering from a failure can be a time-consuming process, often requiring a complete reinstall of the OS or applications. However, in a virtualized environment, snapshots provide an efficient and quick recovery method. Since the VM is simply reverted to a previous state rather than going through a full recovery process, the restoration can often be completed in a matter of minutes, significantly reducing downtime and allowing users or services to resume operations quickly. This is particularly important in production environments where service interruptions need to be minimized to avoid business disruptions.

Restoring a VM from a snapshot is also beneficial for testing and development scenarios. Developers and testers often need to experiment with different configurations, install and uninstall software, or test new updates and features. Snapshots enable them to create a safe environment in which they can try out changes without worrying about permanently altering the system. If the test results are not as expected or if an error occurs, the VM can simply be restored to its prior state. This allows for rapid iteration, experimentation, and testing, as developers can quickly roll back to a known good state and continue their work. Snapshots provide a flexible and non-disruptive way to ensure that testing does not interfere with the overall environment and that developers can proceed with their tasks without the need to constantly reconfigure their systems.

The restoration process from snapshots is straightforward, but it is essential to understand the potential implications of using snapshots as a restoration method. While snapshots capture a point-in-time copy of a VM, they do not necessarily protect against all types of failures. For example, if a snapshot was taken before a system failure or data corruption occurred, restoring the VM to that snapshot will also restore the system to its pre-failure state. This could result in the reappearance of the same issue if the underlying problem was not resolved prior to the restoration. Therefore, before restoring a VM, it is important to diagnose the issue and ensure that the root cause is addressed to prevent the problem from recurring after the restoration. In some cases, restoring a VM from a snapshot may also overwrite data or configurations that were added after the snapshot was taken, so administrators need to carefully consider the impact on data integrity and ensure that no important information is lost during the process.

Another important aspect of restoring virtual machines from snapshots is the potential performance impact. While snapshots provide a fast and efficient way to revert to a previous state, they can introduce some overhead, particularly when multiple snapshots are taken over time. As each snapshot creates a delta file that tracks changes to the VM, the more snapshots there are, the larger the delta files become, and the more resources are required to manage them. If too many snapshots are retained or if they are not properly consolidated, the performance of the virtual machine can degrade. This is especially true in environments where snapshots are frequently created and used for long-term storage. It is important to manage snapshots carefully by consolidating them when no longer needed or by deleting obsolete snapshots to maintain the performance and health of the virtualized environment.

Restoring a VM from a snapshot can also have implications for storage management. When a snapshot is created, it consumes additional disk space because the hypervisor must store the original disk state and track all changes made since the snapshot. If snapshots are retained for extended periods, they can consume a significant amount of storage space, especially if the virtual machines are running resource-intensive applications or generating large amounts of data. To prevent storage from becoming overused, administrators should regularly review the snapshots and delete those that are no longer needed. Additionally, many hypervisors provide options to consolidate snapshots into a single disk file, which helps reduce storage consumption and maintain the VM's disk integrity.

In virtualized environments, snapshots should be used as part of a broader backup and recovery strategy. While snapshots provide a quick and efficient recovery method, they are not a substitute for a comprehensive backup plan. Snapshots are best suited for short-term recovery needs, such as rolling back a VM to a previous state after an update or change, but for long-term data protection, it is essential to use a dedicated backup solution. Regular backups should be taken to ensure that data is preserved beyond the lifespan of the snapshot and can be recovered in the event of a disaster, such as hardware failure or data corruption. Combining snapshots with robust backup practices ensures that virtualized environments remain secure and resilient to data loss.

In some cases, it may be necessary to restore a virtual machine from a snapshot in a cloud environment or across different physical hosts. Many hypervisors and cloud platforms support live migration and snapshot-based replication, allowing administrators to move VMs and their associated snapshots between different hosts or data centers. This feature is especially useful in cloud environments where workloads need to be scaled or moved across different geographical regions. By restoring a VM from a snapshot on a new host, administrators can ensure that the VM remains operational and continues to function as expected, with minimal disruption.

Restoring virtual machines from snapshots is an essential function in virtualized environments, providing a reliable and efficient way to recover from system failures, troubleshoot issues, and test changes. Whether used in development, production, or disaster recovery scenarios, snapshots allow administrators to quickly return to a known good state and minimize downtime. However, effective snapshot management requires careful consideration of storage usage, performance impact, and data integrity to ensure that the benefits of snapshots are fully realized without introducing risks or inefficiencies into the system. By understanding the processes and best practices for snapshot restoration, administrators can leverage this technology to maintain the stability, performance, and resilience of virtualized environments.

Using Snapshots for Disaster Recovery

Snapshots are an essential component of modern disaster recovery strategies in virtualized environments. The ability to quickly restore virtual machines (VMs) to a previous known state is a valuable tool for maintaining business continuity in the event of a system failure, data corruption, or other unforeseen events that could disrupt normal operations. Snapshots capture the exact state of a VM at a specific point in time, including its disk, memory, and configuration. By leveraging snapshots as part of a disaster recovery plan, organizations can ensure that their virtual machines can be quickly restored to a stable, functional state, minimizing downtime and the impact on business operations.

The primary advantage of using snapshots for disaster recovery is the speed at which a system can be restored. Unlike traditional backup methods, which often require a full recovery process involving restoring multiple files and configurations, snapshots capture a full image of the virtual machine at the moment the snapshot is taken. This includes not only the data stored on the virtual disk but also the system settings and the running state of the machine, including active memory. This ability to restore a VM to a specific point in time allows for rapid recovery, even in the event of a critical failure. When a disaster strikes, such as a system crash or a software error that disrupts operations, administrators can restore the VM from a snapshot in a matter of minutes, reducing downtime and allowing business processes to resume as quickly as possible.

Snapshots offer a high degree of flexibility in disaster recovery scenarios. For example, snapshots can be taken before performing system updates, software installations, or configuration changes, allowing administrators to easily revert to a stable state if the changes cause issues. This is particularly useful in environments where changes are made frequently, and the risk of system instability is high. By taking regular snapshots, administrators create a set of restore points that can be used for rollback, minimizing the risk of extended downtime or service interruptions. This proactive approach to disaster recovery ensures that systems remain resilient and can quickly recover from unexpected failures, whether caused by human error, application bugs, or system malfunctions.

One of the most significant benefits of using snapshots in disaster recovery is the reduction in the need for traditional, full-scale backup solutions. While snapshots are not a replacement for long-term backups, they provide a fast and efficient method of recovery for short-term data loss or system failures. Traditional backups often require considerable time to perform, especially in large environments with numerous systems. Restoring data from traditional backups also requires a significant amount of time, as it involves identifying and restoring individual files or system images. Snapshots, on the other hand, allow for near-instantaneous recovery of an entire virtual machine, including its configuration and data, which is crucial for minimizing downtime and restoring operations quickly.

In addition to providing fast recovery, snapshots also offer a high level of granularity in disaster recovery. Administrators can take snapshots at various points in time, capturing the state of the virtual machine at different stages of operation. This provides a set of recovery points that can be used to restore a VM to any of the previous states captured by the snapshots. This flexibility is particularly valuable in complex virtualized environments where different VMs may be running different workloads or operating systems. For example, a VM running a critical database application can be restored to a snapshot taken just before a database upgrade, ensuring that the system can return to its previous working state without the need to manually roll back changes or troubleshoot the issues caused by the upgrade.

Snapshots are also an essential tool in maintaining high availability and fault tolerance in virtualized environments. In environments where multiple VMs are running on a single host or across a cluster of hosts, snapshots provide a method for preserving the state of VMs in real time. If a failure occurs in one of the VMs, administrators can restore it to a snapshot taken before the failure, allowing the VM to continue running without significant disruption. This is especially important in cloud environments or multi-tenant data centers, where the availability of VMs is critical for maintaining service levels and meeting customer expectations. By using snapshots in conjunction with other high availability features, such as live migration and automatic failover, administrators can ensure that VMs can be quickly restored to a working state in the event of a failure, reducing the likelihood of downtime and service interruptions.

Despite their many advantages, the use of snapshots for disaster recovery also requires careful management to ensure their effectiveness. Over time, the number of snapshots retained can grow, consuming significant amounts of storage space. If not managed properly, this can lead to storage shortages and negatively impact system performance. Additionally, excessive use of snapshots can result in performance degradation, as the hypervisor must manage the changes made to the VM after the snapshot was taken. This can create overhead that impacts the VM's overall performance, particularly when dealing with resource-intensive workloads. To mitigate these risks, administrators should implement policies to manage snapshots effectively, including regularly deleting outdated snapshots, consolidating snapshots when appropriate, and ensuring that only necessary snapshots are retained for recovery purposes.

Another consideration when using snapshots for disaster recovery is the potential for data inconsistency. While snapshots capture the entire state of a virtual machine, including its disk and memory, they may not always capture the state of in-flight transactions or data changes that occur during the snapshot process. This is particularly true in scenarios where a VM is running transactional applications, such as databases or financial systems. To address this, administrators should ensure that applications are quiesced or paused before taking a snapshot to ensure that data consistency is maintained. Many hypervisors provide tools to integrate with application-level quiescing mechanisms, ensuring that the snapshot captures a consistent state of the application and its data.

In environments where frequent snapshots are taken for disaster recovery purposes, administrators should also ensure that snapshot schedules do not conflict with other backup processes or system maintenance tasks. Coordination between snapshots and other backup mechanisms is essential to prevent conflicts, such as taking a snapshot while a backup is in progress, which could result in inconsistent or incomplete data. To avoid such issues, administrators should carefully plan snapshot schedules and ensure that they are integrated with the broader disaster recovery strategy.

Using snapshots for disaster recovery provides an efficient and flexible method for protecting virtualized environments against system failures, data corruption, and other unforeseen events. By capturing the state of virtual machines at specific points in time, snapshots allow for rapid recovery, minimal downtime, and easy rollback to previous configurations. While snapshots offer significant benefits, their effective use requires careful planning, storage management, and integration with other recovery mechanisms. With the right strategies in place, snapshots become an invaluable tool in maintaining business continuity and ensuring that virtualized systems can recover quickly and efficiently from disasters.

Virtual Machine Cloning and Templates

Virtual machine cloning and templates are two powerful features in virtualized environments that enhance efficiency, scalability, and ease of management. Both methods streamline the process of creating and deploying virtual machines, but they serve different purposes and offer distinct advantages in different use cases. Cloning refers to the process of creating an exact copy of an existing virtual machine, while templates provide a pre-configured, reusable base image of a virtual machine that can be deployed as needed. Both techniques are central to modern IT infrastructures, particularly in cloud computing and large-scale virtualized environments, where rapid provisioning of virtual machines is essential to meet growing demands.

Cloning a virtual machine involves creating an identical copy of an existing VM, including its operating system, applications, data, and configuration settings. This process is beneficial when administrators need to quickly create additional VMs with the same configuration and setup as an existing one. For example, in a development environment, when multiple developers require identical testing environments, cloning an existing VM saves time and effort compared to setting up each VM from scratch. Once cloned, the new VM operates independently of the original, allowing for modifications or customizations specific to its intended use case. Cloning is particularly useful when multiple similar VMs are needed for various tasks, such as testing different software configurations or scaling up resources to meet high demand.

The cloning process is relatively simple and typically involves a few key steps. First, the source VM is selected, and the cloning operation is initiated. During this process, the hypervisor creates a copy of the source VM's virtual disks, memory, and configuration settings, and a new virtual machine is created based on these elements. Depending on the hypervisor or platform in use, the cloned VM may or may not be powered on immediately after the process is complete. After cloning, administrators can customize the new VM, such as changing its network settings, allocating different hardware resources, or modifying the operating system configuration. Cloning can be done either as a full clone, where the new VM is entirely independent of the original, or as a linked clone, where the new VM shares a portion of the original VM's disk and configuration, which saves storage space but may introduce dependencies.

One of the primary benefits of cloning is its efficiency in scaling virtualized environments. In cloud computing platforms, where on-demand provisioning of VMs is critical, cloning allows administrators to quickly scale resources by deploying new VMs that mirror the configurations of existing ones. This is especially valuable in environments where workloads can change rapidly and require the addition of new virtual machines with minimal effort. For example, if a cloud service provider needs to quickly add additional virtual machines to handle an increase in user demand, cloning an existing VM with the same configuration allows for faster provisioning compared to manually setting up new VMs from scratch.

While cloning is an excellent solution for creating additional virtual machines quickly, templates provide a more efficient and scalable way to deploy standardized virtual machines across an organization. A template is essentially a master image of a virtual machine that has been pre-configured with an operating system, applications, and settings that are required for specific tasks or workloads. Unlike cloning, which creates an identical copy of an existing VM, a template serves as a blueprint that can be used to create multiple VMs with a consistent configuration. Templates are often used to streamline the process of deploying new VMs, ensuring that they are configured according to organizational standards and best practices.

Templates are particularly useful in large-scale environments where consistency is key. For example, in an enterprise environment, it is essential that all virtual machines running critical applications or services are configured in a standardized way to ensure compatibility, security, and ease of management. By creating a template with the necessary configurations and software, administrators can deploy new VMs that are guaranteed to meet these requirements, reducing the risk of configuration errors and streamlining the deployment process. Templates are also commonly used in environments where VMs are deployed on a large scale, such as in cloud services or managed hosting environments, where hundreds or thousands of virtual machines may need to be provisioned.

Creating a template involves several steps, including the configuration of the VM's operating system, installation of necessary software, and application of security settings and updates. Once the VM is fully configured, it is converted into a template by the hypervisor. The template itself does not store data specific to any one VM, such as user files or application data, but instead focuses on the core configuration and system image. This allows for efficient storage and deployment of new virtual machines based on the template, while maintaining consistency across all instances. When a new VM is deployed from a template, it is essentially an exact copy of the configuration defined in the template, allowing for quick and standardized provisioning of new virtual machines.

Another significant advantage of using templates is the ability to automate VM provisioning. In many virtualized environments, templates are integrated into orchestration and automation tools, which allow administrators to define policies for automatic VM creation based on specific criteria. For example, if a new application needs to be deployed, an automation tool can trigger the creation of a new VM from a specific template, ensuring that the VM is configured with the necessary resources and software. This reduces the need for manual intervention and ensures that new VMs are deployed consistently and efficiently. The automation of VM provisioning is particularly beneficial in dynamic environments, such as cloud platforms, where resources need to be allocated quickly to meet changing demands.

While templates are invaluable for deploying standardized VMs, they are not as flexible as cloning when it comes to creating VMs with custom configurations. Since a template is designed to provide a predefined configuration, any changes to the template may require the creation of a new one. If a specific VM requires additional customizations or deviations from the template configuration, cloning the original VM may be a better option. However, templates can be updated periodically, with new versions being created to reflect changes in software or configuration requirements.

Despite the differences between cloning and templates, both techniques can be used together to enhance the efficiency and scalability of virtualized environments. For example, administrators can create a base VM with a specific configuration and software stack, then use that base VM to create templates for standardized deployments. If a specific VM configuration is needed for a particular task, administrators can clone the base VM and modify it as necessary. This combination of cloning and templates allows for greater flexibility and control in virtualized environments, ensuring that VMs can be deployed quickly, efficiently, and in a standardized manner.

Virtual machine cloning and templates are integral to the management and scalability of virtualized systems. Cloning allows administrators to quickly replicate existing VMs, providing a fast method for scaling resources and creating additional instances. Templates, on the other hand, offer a way to deploy standardized, pre-configured VMs that meet organizational requirements, ensuring consistency and reducing the risk of errors. By leveraging both techniques, administrators can optimize their virtualized environments for speed, efficiency, and reliability, making it easier to scale workloads and maintain system consistency across a wide range of applications and services.

Managing Virtual Machine Lifecycle

Managing the lifecycle of virtual machines (VMs) is a critical responsibility in any virtualized infrastructure. The VM lifecycle refers to the series of stages a virtual machine goes through from its creation to its retirement. These stages include provisioning, deployment, operation, maintenance, and decommissioning, with each stage requiring careful management to ensure efficiency, performance, and resource optimization. Effective VM lifecycle management is essential for maintaining the stability, security, and scalability of virtualized environments, especially in data centers or cloud environments where thousands of virtual machines may be running simultaneously.

The first stage of the virtual machine lifecycle is provisioning. This involves creating a new virtual machine, typically from a template or a cloned machine, and allocating the necessary resources, such as CPU, memory, storage, and network interfaces. Provisioning a VM requires selecting the appropriate configuration based on the intended workload and usage requirements. In some environments, this process is automated through orchestration tools or scripts, allowing administrators to quickly spin up new VMs without manual intervention. The provisioning stage may also involve installing the operating system, configuring system settings, and applying security patches to ensure that the VM is ready for use.

Once a VM is provisioned, the next stage in its lifecycle is deployment. During deployment, the VM is made available for use and is integrated into the operational environment. This often involves configuring the network settings so that the VM can communicate with other systems and external resources. In a cloud environment, deployment may also involve registering the VM with the cloud management platform, allowing it to be monitored and managed alongside other VMs. The deployment stage ensures that the virtual machine is fully operational, with all necessary software and resources configured and ready for use.

After deployment, the VM enters the operation phase, where it is actively used to run applications and services. This is typically the longest phase in the VM lifecycle, as the machine continues to operate until it is no longer needed or until it reaches the end of its useful life. During the operation phase, monitoring becomes essential. Administrators need to ensure that the VM has sufficient resources to perform its tasks, and that it is running efficiently. Resource utilization monitoring tools can help track CPU, memory, storage, and network usage, allowing administrators to make adjustments if a VM is consuming more resources than expected or if it requires scaling.

Maintenance is an ongoing part of managing a VM during its operational phase. Maintenance tasks may include applying software updates and patches, upgrading the operating system or applications, and performing routine system checks to ensure that the VM is functioning correctly. Regular maintenance is necessary to address security vulnerabilities, improve performance, and prevent system failures. Administrators may also perform backup and disaster recovery tests during the maintenance phase, ensuring that data is backed up and that the VM can be restored in the event of a failure. The maintenance phase is crucial for extending the life of the VM, as it ensures that the VM remains secure, stable, and efficient throughout its operation.

In virtualized environments, especially those with many VMs, administrators must also be proactive in managing VM resource allocation during the operation phase. VMs often share physical resources with other VMs on the same host, and over time, resource contention can arise, leading to performance degradation. Proper resource management involves ensuring that each VM is allocated enough resources to meet its needs without over-consuming shared resources. This may involve adjusting the VM's allocated CPU or memory, moving the VM to a different host with more available resources, or even decommissioning VMs that are no longer necessary. Tools such as dynamic resource allocation, load balancing, and VM migration are commonly used in virtualized environments to optimize resource utilization and ensure that VMs perform at their best.

The decommissioning phase marks the end of a VM's lifecycle. This stage involves shutting down the VM, removing it from the operational environment, and reclaiming its resources. Decommissioning a VM may occur for several reasons, such as when it is no longer needed, when it is being replaced by a newer VM, or when the VM's workload is being moved to another machine. Before decommissioning, administrators should ensure that all important data is backed up or transferred, and that any dependencies associated with the VM are addressed. For example, if the VM is running critical services, administrators need to ensure that these services are moved or migrated to another VM to avoid service disruptions.

Once the VM has been shut down and its resources reclaimed, the virtual machine is either deleted or archived, depending on the organization's policies. In some cases, VMs may be archived for future use or for regulatory compliance reasons, especially if the VM contains historical data that may be required later. In cloud environments, decommissioned VMs are typically removed from the cloud management platform, ensuring that they no longer consume resources or incur costs. In on-premises environments, decommissioned VMs may be stored for potential reactivation or repurposing, though it is crucial to ensure that data security standards are followed during this process.

Managing the lifecycle of virtual machines also involves addressing security concerns. From the provisioning stage through to decommissioning, ensuring that VMs are secure is a constant task. During the provisioning stage, administrators should follow security best practices, such as setting up firewalls, applying security patches, and configuring access controls. During the operation phase, regular vulnerability assessments and security audits should be performed to identify and mitigate any potential risks. When decommissioning a

VM, it is important to securely erase any sensitive data to prevent unauthorized access, especially if the VM is being disposed of or repurposed for another task. A thorough and consistent approach to security throughout the VM lifecycle helps prevent breaches, data leaks, and other security incidents.

Another critical aspect of managing the VM lifecycle is compliance. Many organizations are subject to regulatory requirements that mandate the retention, handling, and deletion of data in specific ways. Administrators must ensure that VMs containing sensitive or regulated data are handled in compliance with these requirements throughout their lifecycle. This may involve setting up monitoring to track VM activity, ensuring data is encrypted, and making sure that decommissioned VMs are disposed of according to regulatory guidelines.

The lifecycle of virtual machines is complex and requires ongoing management and oversight. From provisioning and deployment to operation and decommissioning, each phase involves specific tasks and responsibilities aimed at ensuring the stability, performance, and security of the virtualized infrastructure. Effective VM lifecycle management is essential for optimizing resource utilization, minimizing downtime, and maintaining compliance with security and regulatory standards. By implementing best practices for each stage of the VM lifecycle, administrators can enhance the efficiency and resilience of virtualized environments, providing a solid foundation for modern IT operations.

Performance Monitoring for Virtual Machines

Performance monitoring for virtual machines (VMs) is a critical practice for maintaining the health and efficiency of virtualized environments. Virtual machines are often part of larger infrastructure ecosystems, such as data centers or cloud platforms, where multiple VMs are running on the same physical hardware. Given that these VMs share resources like CPU, memory, and storage, monitoring their performance is essential to ensure optimal resource allocation, prevent bottlenecks, and identify any issues that may negatively impact system performance. Performance monitoring helps administrators keep track of various metrics, make informed decisions about resource management, and maintain the stability and efficiency of the virtual environment.

The primary goal of performance monitoring in virtualized environments is to ensure that VMs have enough resources to run their workloads efficiently without over-consuming the physical host's resources. Each virtual machine depends on the host for physical resources, including CPU cycles, memory, disk space, and network bandwidth. A VM's performance can be affected by a variety of factors, such as inadequate resource allocation, competition for resources among multiple VMs, or issues within the VM itself. To address these potential problems, administrators need to continuously track the performance of the VMs and the underlying host systems to ensure that all components are functioning optimally.

CPU utilization is one of the key performance metrics to monitor in virtual machines. The CPU is the central processing unit that drives most of the processing tasks in a VM. Virtual machines are typically assigned a number of virtual CPUs (vCPUs), which are mapped to physical CPU cores on the host machine. Monitoring CPU usage helps administrators understand whether a VM is being allocated enough processing power or if it is competing with other VMs for CPU resources. High CPU utilization can indicate that a VM is running resource-intensive applications, which could lead to slower performance if the VM is not allocated sufficient resources. Conversely, low CPU usage may suggest that the VM is underutilized, leading to inefficiencies in resource allocation. CPU usage must be balanced carefully to avoid both underprovisioning and overprovisioning, both of which can impact the overall performance of the virtualized environment.

Memory management is another crucial area of performance monitoring. Virtual machines rely on virtual memory, which is mapped to the physical memory of the host system. When a VM's memory utilization exceeds its allocation, the hypervisor may need to swap or balloon memory from the host, which can slow down performance.

Memory overcommitment, where the total virtual memory assigned to all VMs exceeds the physical memory available on the host, can lead to increased latency and poor performance. Conversely, underutilized memory may indicate inefficiency, as it could be allocated to VMs that do not require it. Monitoring memory usage allows administrators to adjust allocations dynamically, ensuring that each VM has access to the resources it needs while avoiding excessive memory consumption that could negatively impact the overall performance of the host system.

Disk I/O is another vital performance metric to monitor for virtual machines. Virtual disks in VMs are essentially files stored on the host's physical storage system, and their performance can be significantly impacted by storage I/O. High disk utilization can lead to slow read and write operations, affecting the performance of applications and services running within the VM. Disk I/O bottlenecks may arise from resource contention, where multiple VMs are competing for access to the same physical storage resources. Monitoring disk I/O performance helps identify these bottlenecks, enabling administrators to adjust the storage configuration or allocate more resources to specific VMs that require high-performance storage. Virtualized environments often rely on storage solutions like shared storage area networks (SANs) or network-attached storage (NAS), and performance monitoring is essential for ensuring that these systems provide sufficient throughput to meet the demands of the VMs.

Network performance is equally important to track in virtualized environments. Virtual machines rely on virtual network interfaces to communicate with each other and external resources. Monitoring network utilization helps ensure that VMs are not experiencing congestion or latency due to insufficient bandwidth or network misconfigurations. Network bottlenecks can occur when multiple VMs share the same physical network resources, leading to slower communication and potentially affecting application performance. Administrators must monitor network traffic to ensure that VMs are not overwhelming the network, leading to delays or disruptions in service. Furthermore, by tracking network traffic, administrators can ensure that VMs are securely isolated from each other and prevent unauthorized access to sensitive data.

In virtualized environments, resource contention between VMs is a common challenge that administrators must address. When multiple VMs are running on the same physical host, they share the host's resources, which can lead to competition for CPU, memory, storage, and network bandwidth. Monitoring resource usage across all VMs helps administrators identify when a VM is consuming more resources than necessary, potentially affecting the performance of other VMs. Load balancing and resource allocation strategies can help mitigate these issues, ensuring that resources are distributed equitably among all running VMs. Resource management tools often allow administrators to set resource limits or priorities, ensuring that critical VMs receive the necessary resources without being impacted by less critical workloads.

The performance of the hypervisor itself also needs to be monitored. The hypervisor is the underlying software responsible for managing the virtual machines and allocating resources to them. Hypervisor performance can impact the performance of the entire virtualized environment, especially if it is overburdened with too many VMs or running inefficiently. Monitoring hypervisor health, including its CPU, memory, and storage usage, is essential to ensure that the underlying system can support the demands of the VMs running on it. Hypervisor performance can also be influenced by factors such as the host system's hardware capabilities, network configurations, and storage subsystems. Administrators need to track the health of the hypervisor to identify any potential issues before they impact the VMs it manages.

Advanced performance monitoring tools in virtualized environments often provide real-time monitoring dashboards, alerting systems, and detailed logs that allow administrators to track performance metrics continuously. These tools can offer insights into CPU and memory usage, storage I/O, network traffic, and hypervisor performance, all in real-time. Administrators can set thresholds for each performance metric, triggering alerts when those thresholds are exceeded. These alerts can help identify performance degradation, potential bottlenecks, or resource shortages before they affect the operation of the VMs. Additionally, performance logs allow administrators to track performance trends over time, which can help with capacity planning and predicting future resource needs.

Regular performance monitoring is essential not only for ensuring that VMs are running optimally but also for proactive problem-solving. Identifying performance bottlenecks early allows administrators to take corrective action before problems escalate, preventing service interruptions or prolonged downtimes. For example, if a VM consistently experiences high CPU utilization, administrators may choose to allocate additional resources, move the VM to a different host with more capacity, or optimize the workload to reduce the demand. Similarly, high memory usage can be addressed by reallocating resources or implementing memory management techniques such as memory ballooning or swapping.

Performance monitoring for virtual machines is crucial for ensuring the efficiency, stability, and scalability of virtualized environments. By tracking key metrics such as CPU utilization, memory usage, disk I/O, and network performance, administrators can optimize resource allocation, prevent bottlenecks, and maintain the overall health of the virtualized infrastructure. Continuous monitoring and proactive management are necessary to ensure that VMs perform efficiently and meet the demands of users and applications. By leveraging advanced monitoring tools and strategies, administrators can ensure that their virtualized environments are running at peak performance and avoid the negative impacts of performance issues.

Troubleshooting Virtual Machine Issues

Virtual machines (VMs) are central to modern IT infrastructure, providing flexibility, scalability, and isolation. However, like any other technology, they are not immune to issues that can affect their performance and stability. Troubleshooting virtual machine issues is an essential skill for administrators managing virtualized environments, especially when these issues can disrupt business operations, cause downtime, or lead to data loss. The challenges associated with virtual machine troubleshooting arise from the complexity of the virtualized environment, where hardware and software resources are abstracted and shared across multiple VMs. Identifying and resolving issues in such environments requires a systematic approach, a deep understanding of the underlying infrastructure, and effective diagnostic tools.

One of the most common issues faced in virtualized environments is resource contention. VMs share the physical resources of the host system, including CPU, memory, disk, and network interfaces. When multiple VMs are running on the same host, resource contention can occur if the resources are not allocated effectively. For example, a virtual machine may experience poor performance if it is allocated insufficient CPU or memory resources, or if it is competing with other VMs for the same resources. Troubleshooting this type of issue begins with monitoring resource utilization, identifying which VMs are consuming excessive resources, and understanding whether the host system is overloaded. Administrators can use hypervisor tools or third-party monitoring software to check CPU, memory, disk, and network usage. If resource contention is detected, solutions may include adjusting resource allocations, such as increasing the number of virtual CPUs or memory allocated to a VM, or moving VMs to other hosts with more available resources.

Another common issue is VM performance degradation, which can manifest as slow application response times, delayed network communication, or unresponsive systems. This issue can be caused by several factors, including inadequate resource allocation, poor disk I/O performance, or excessive network latency. When troubleshooting performance degradation, it is important to examine both the VM and the underlying host. Resource overcommitment on the host system, where more resources are allocated to VMs than the physical hardware can support, can lead to performance issues. Monitoring tools can help identify whether CPU, memory, or storage I/O is causing the problem. For example, if disk I/O is slow, it may be necessary to optimize the storage system or ensure that the VM is not overusing disk resources. Additionally, network issues, such as bandwidth limitations or configuration errors, can lead to slow performance. Checking the VM's network configuration and monitoring the network for congestion or errors can help identify and resolve these issues.

In some cases, VMs may fail to start, which can be a serious issue in production environments. When troubleshooting VM startup issues, it is important to check the VM's configuration and the status of its virtual hardware. The hypervisor's logs can provide valuable information about the root cause of the problem, such as whether there are issues with the virtual disk, the VM's configuration file, or the hypervisor itself. Common causes of VM startup failures include corruption of the VM's virtual disk or configuration files, insufficient resources, or conflicts between the VM and the host system. A thorough examination of the VM's configuration settings, including the allocation of virtual CPUs, memory, and storage, can help identify any discrepancies or misconfigurations that may prevent the VM from starting. Additionally, administrators should verify that the host system has enough available resources to support the VM's startup process.

Another area of concern when troubleshooting virtual machine issues is network connectivity. VMs rely on virtual network adapters to communicate with other VMs and external resources. Network issues can arise when there are problems with the virtual network adapter, the virtual switch, or the underlying physical network. Common network issues include misconfigured network settings, VLAN mismatches, or problems with the virtual switch configuration. Troubleshooting network connectivity issues requires checking the VM's network configuration, including the IP address, subnet mask, gateway, and DNS settings. It is also important to verify that the virtual switch is properly configured and that it is connected to the correct physical network interface on the host system. If the issue persists, administrators should check for any issues with the physical network infrastructure, such as network cables, switches, or routers that may be causing the connectivity problem.

VM snapshot and backup issues can also cause significant problems, especially if snapshots are not properly managed or if backup operations fail. Snapshots are useful for preserving the state of a VM at a specific point in time, but they can introduce complications if not managed carefully. If a snapshot is not deleted or consolidated after it is no longer needed, it can consume significant storage space and degrade the performance of the VM. Additionally, if multiple snapshots are created over time without consolidation, the VM's performance may suffer due to the overhead associated with managing the snapshots. Administrators should regularly review and delete unnecessary snapshots to ensure that storage is used efficiently and that performance is not impacted. Backup failures can also occur when there are issues with the backup software, storage devices, or network connectivity. When troubleshooting backup issues, it is important to check the backup logs, verify that the backup destination is accessible, and ensure that the backup process is not being interrupted by network or storage issues.

Security-related issues are another important aspect of virtual machine troubleshooting. VMs can be vulnerable to security threats just like physical machines, and problems can arise if a VM becomes compromised, if there are security misconfigurations, or if patches are not applied in a timely manner. When troubleshooting security issues, administrators should review the VM's security settings, such as firewalls, antivirus software, and access control lists (ACLs). Additionally, administrators should ensure that the latest security patches are installed and that the VM is not running outdated or vulnerable software. If a VM is compromised, it is important to identify the source of the breach, contain the threat, and restore the VM to a known secure state. Administrators should also consider implementing monitoring tools to detect potential security incidents and ensure that VMs remain secure over time.

In virtualized environments, ensuring the health of the hypervisor and the underlying physical hardware is also crucial for troubleshooting VM issues. The hypervisor is the layer of software that manages the virtual machines, and if it becomes unstable or fails, it can affect the performance and availability of all the VMs running on it. Regularly checking the status of the hypervisor, reviewing system logs, and monitoring hardware health can help identify potential issues before they impact the VMs. In addition, hardware failures, such as failing disks, memory, or network adapters on the host system, can cause VM performance degradation or even downtime. Administrators should implement hardware monitoring tools to ensure that the underlying infrastructure remains reliable.

Troubleshooting virtual machine issues requires a methodical approach, an understanding of both the virtualized and physical infrastructure, and the use of monitoring and diagnostic tools. Virtual machines are critical to modern IT operations, and resolving issues quickly is essential to maintaining system uptime and performance. By identifying the root causes of VM problems—whether related to resource allocation, network connectivity, snapshots, security, or the underlying hypervisor—administrators can ensure that virtualized environments remain stable, secure, and efficient.

Migration: Live and Offline Methods

Migration is a crucial process in virtualized environments, enabling the movement of virtual machines (VMs) from one physical host to another or from one data center to another. The ability to migrate VMs efficiently ensures that workloads can be balanced, hardware resources can be optimized, and downtime can be minimized. There are two primary methods of VM migration: live migration and offline migration. Both methods offer distinct advantages and are used in different scenarios based on the needs of the organization. Live migration allows a VM to continue running while being moved to a different host, while offline migration involves shutting down the VM before it is moved. Understanding both methods and knowing when to apply them is key to optimizing the management of virtualized environments.

Live migration is a method that enables the movement of a virtual machine from one physical host to another without interrupting the VM's operation. This is particularly important in environments where high availability and minimal downtime are essential, such as in production systems, cloud computing platforms, or large-scale data centers. During live migration, the VM's memory, CPU state, storage, and network connections are transferred to the target host in real-time, ensuring that the VM continues to operate as if it had never been moved. Live migration is typically supported by hypervisors such as VMware vSphere, Microsoft Hyper-V, and others, which provide the necessary tools and protocols to facilitate the migration process.

The main benefit of live migration is that it allows administrators to move VMs without impacting the end users or applications running on the machine. This is particularly useful for load balancing, where VMs are moved to different hosts to optimize resource utilization. For instance, if one host is under heavy load while others are underutilized, live migration can be used to redistribute VMs to ensure that all physical hosts are operating at peak efficiency. Similarly, during hardware maintenance or upgrades, live migration enables administrators to move VMs from one host to another, allowing for maintenance work without causing disruptions to running services. The ability to perform live migration without service interruption enhances the overall flexibility and availability of virtualized infrastructures.

Live migration also plays an important role in disaster recovery and business continuity planning. In the event of a host failure or other unexpected events, live migration can be used to transfer the VM to another host in real-time, ensuring that services remain operational. In a cloud environment, this capability allows for the seamless movement of workloads across data centers, providing fault tolerance and high availability. Since the migration process occurs while the VM is still running, there is no need for manual intervention or downtime, making it an efficient solution for maintaining service continuity.

However, live migration does come with some challenges. One of the primary concerns is the need for shared storage. During the migration process, the VM's storage must be accessible from both the source and destination hosts. This requires the use of shared storage systems, such as a Storage Area Network (SAN) or Network-Attached Storage (NAS), to ensure that the VM's disk data can be accessed by both hosts without interruption. In addition, the hypervisor must ensure that the VM's network connectivity is maintained during the migration process. Network configurations must be compatible on both the source and destination hosts, and the VM must retain its IP address and other network settings throughout the move.

Another potential issue with live migration is the impact on system performance. While the migration is in progress, there may be a brief period where the VM experiences performance degradation due to the overhead associated with transferring its memory and state. In environments with high-performance workloads or limited resources, this can lead to temporary slowdowns. Therefore, administrators must carefully monitor system resources and network bandwidth to ensure that the live migration process does not negatively affect the performance of other VMs or critical applications.

Offline migration, on the other hand, involves shutting down the VM before it is moved to a new host. This method is typically used when live migration is not possible or when the VM's configuration requires it. For example, offline migration may be used when the VM's storage is not compatible with shared storage solutions or when network configurations cannot be preserved during migration. Offline migration can also be a simpler and more reliable method when it comes to moving VMs between hosts that are not part of the same virtualized cluster or when the VM needs to be reconfigured in some way as part of the migration.

The primary advantage of offline migration is that it avoids the challenges associated with live migration, such as maintaining network connectivity and ensuring access to shared storage. Since the VM is shut down during the migration, there is no need to worry about the complexities of transferring memory or handling active processes. The VM is simply powered off, moved to the new host, and then powered on again. This simplicity makes offline migration a more straightforward option in certain scenarios, especially when the VM needs to be relocated to a different physical infrastructure or when there are concerns about system performance during migration.

However, the major downside of offline migration is the downtime involved. Since the VM must be powered off before the migration can occur, any services or applications running on the VM will experience interruption. For production systems that require high availability, this downtime can be unacceptable. Offline migration is therefore typically used in non-production environments or in situations where the VM can afford some downtime, such as when performing maintenance or moving a VM between different physical environments that require reconfiguration.

Both live and offline migration are essential tools for managing virtualized environments, and each has its advantages and trade-offs. Live migration is best suited for environments where uptime and high availability are critical. It enables administrators to move VMs between hosts without interrupting services, making it ideal for load balancing, disaster recovery, and hardware maintenance. On the other hand, offline migration is a simpler and more reliable method that can be used in situations where downtime is acceptable or when shared storage is not available. While offline migration may cause some disruption, it remains an effective option for relocating VMs that need to be reconfigured or moved between different infrastructures.

When deciding between live and offline migration, administrators must consider factors such as the type of workload, the impact of downtime, available resources, and the complexity of the virtualized environment. For example, in a cloud environment where workloads must scale rapidly to meet fluctuating demand, live migration is often the preferred method to ensure seamless resource allocation and minimal service disruption. In contrast, offline migration may be more appropriate when dealing with legacy systems or in situations where the virtual machine needs to be moved between different storage systems that do not support live migration.

Effective migration strategies also require careful planning and testing. Administrators should evaluate the performance of live migration in their environments and ensure that shared storage, network configurations, and resource availability are properly configured to minimize any potential issues. Similarly, offline migration requires planning for downtime and ensuring that the VM's data is safely transferred and backed up during the migration process. By understanding the strengths and limitations of both live and offline migration methods, administrators can make informed decisions to ensure that VMs are moved efficiently and with minimal disruption.

VM Resource Overcommitment and Balancing

Resource overcommitment and balancing are two critical concepts in virtualized environments that allow administrators to maximize the efficiency and utilization of their infrastructure. Virtualization inherently involves sharing physical resources—such as CPU, memory, and storage—across multiple virtual machines (VMs) that run on the same physical host. While this allows for higher resource density and better overall resource usage, it also introduces challenges, particularly when VMs are allocated more resources than the physical host can support. This phenomenon, known as resource overcommitment, can be a double-edged sword; when managed correctly, it leads to increased resource efficiency, but if handled improperly, it can result in performance degradation and instability.

VM resource overcommitment occurs when the total virtual resources allocated to the VMs exceed the physical resources available on the host system. In simple terms, administrators assign more virtual CPUs (vCPUs), memory, or storage to VMs than are available on the host. This practice is particularly common in environments where not all VMs use their full resource allocation at all times, such as in development, testing, or other non-production environments where workloads are variable. Overcommitting resources can provide significant benefits, such as cost savings and improved resource utilization. By taking advantage of idle CPU cycles, unused memory, and other unutilized resources, administrators can run more VMs on a given host than would be possible with a 1:1 resource allocation, thereby increasing density and reducing hardware costs.

The primary benefit of resource overcommitment is its ability to maximize the potential of available resources. In traditional physical systems, each server is often allocated a fixed amount of CPU, memory, and storage, which may lead to inefficiencies if the system is underutilized. However, in a virtualized environment, overcommitting resources allows for more efficient use of the physical hardware, as not all VMs will require their full allocation at all times. For example, a VM might only use 50% of its allocated memory or CPU during periods of low workload, but that resource is still reserved for the VM, preventing other VMs from using it. By overcommitting memory and CPU, administrators can ensure that the physical host is running at higher capacity, reducing the need for additional hardware and lowering costs.

However, while resource overcommitment can lead to efficiency gains, it can also introduce risks. One of the primary challenges of overcommitting resources is that it can lead to resource contention. When multiple VMs require more resources than are physically available on the host, performance issues arise. For instance, if the CPU or memory utilization reaches a threshold where resources are insufficient, VMs may experience slowdowns or even failures. In memory overcommitment scenarios, where more virtual memory is allocated than is physically available, the hypervisor may resort to swapping memory to disk or using techniques like ballooning, which introduces latency and performance overhead. CPU overcommitment can lead to excessive context switching, where the hypervisor has to manage the distribution of CPU time between multiple VMs, further impacting performance. In such cases, administrators may observe slower application response times, delays, or even system crashes, especially if the overcommitment is too aggressive.

To manage resource overcommitment effectively, administrators must implement a careful balancing strategy. Resource balancing involves ensuring that each VM is allocated the appropriate amount of resources based on its needs and usage patterns. This requires understanding the workloads of individual VMs and how they interact with shared resources. Ideally, resource allocation should be dynamic and adjust based on the real-time demands of each VM. Balancing ensures that no single VM consumes an excessive share of the host's resources while still providing adequate resources to all VMs. In practice, this can be achieved through several techniques, such as resource limits, affinity rules, and dynamic resource scheduling.

Resource limits can be applied to ensure that VMs do not exceed their allocated CPU, memory, or storage. Setting resource limits helps prevent a single VM from monopolizing resources, ensuring fair distribution among all VMs on the host. For example, administrators can limit the maximum amount of CPU time or memory that a VM can consume, preventing it from impacting the performance of other VMs. Affinity rules, on the other hand, allow administrators to control which VMs run on which physical hosts. By setting affinity rules, administrators can prevent resource contention between specific VMs or ensure that VMs with similar resource demands are placed on the same host for better performance.

Dynamic resource scheduling is another essential technique for balancing resources in a virtualized environment. Hypervisors like VMware vSphere and Microsoft Hyper-V use dynamic resource scheduling algorithms to automatically balance resource allocation across hosts in a cluster. This ensures that VMs are moved to different hosts based on their current resource needs and the available capacity of the physical hosts. Dynamic resource scheduling helps prevent resource exhaustion on a single host by redistributing VMs to underutilized hosts in the cluster. This process can be done manually or automatically, depending on the configuration, and is especially useful in large-scale environments where VMs are constantly being added, removed, or rebalanced.

To optimize resource balancing, administrators must regularly monitor the resource usage of VMs and hosts. Tools like performance monitoring dashboards, resource utilization reports, and alerting systems can provide valuable insights into how resources are being consumed. Monitoring helps administrators identify potential issues early, such as resource contention or underutilization, allowing them to make informed decisions about VM migration, resource adjustments, or overcommitment policies. Performance monitoring tools also help in tracking trends, enabling administrators to predict future resource needs and avoid overcommitment that could result in performance degradation.

While balancing resources across VMs is essential, the physical hardware of the host system also plays a crucial role in the overall performance. Modern hypervisors provide features like NUMA (Non-Uniform Memory Access) optimization and processor affinity to ensure that memory and CPU resources are allocated efficiently across multi-core systems. In multi-CPU systems, NUMA-aware resource scheduling ensures that VMs running on the same host can access memory more efficiently by allocating memory from the same NUMA node. Processor affinity ensures that VMs are assigned to specific physical CPU cores, optimizing performance by reducing the overhead caused by CPU migration. These advanced techniques improve resource allocation and help administrators make the best use of available physical hardware.

Finally, balancing resource overcommitment requires a strategic approach to scaling virtualized environments. As workloads grow and the number of VMs increases, administrators must plan for future capacity needs. Scaling up a virtualized environment involves adding additional physical hosts, increasing storage capacity, or upgrading network infrastructure to support the increasing demand for resources. Capacity planning tools and predictive analytics can help administrators forecast resource needs based on current usage patterns and historical data, ensuring that resources are scaled appropriately before issues arise.

Resource overcommitment and balancing are key elements of managing a virtualized environment. While overcommitment can provide significant efficiency gains and cost savings, it requires careful monitoring and management to avoid resource contention and performance issues. Balancing resources ensures that VMs receive the resources they need without overwhelming the physical host. By using a combination of techniques, including resource limits, dynamic scheduling, and monitoring, administrators can achieve an optimal balance between efficiency and performance in virtualized environments. Through careful management of resource allocation, virtualized infrastructures can scale effectively, providing high levels of performance and availability to support the demands of modern workloads.

High Availability in Virtualized Environments

High availability (HA) in virtualized environments refers to the ability to ensure continuous operation of virtual machines (VMs) and applications, even in the face of hardware failures, system crashes, or other unforeseen events that could otherwise cause service interruptions. In a virtualized environment, where multiple VMs run on a single physical host, the need for high availability is especially critical to maintain business continuity. Virtualization introduces both advantages and challenges in ensuring that applications and workloads remain available, and the techniques used to achieve high availability are a key part of modern data center management.

One of the main advantages of virtualization in providing high availability is the ability to consolidate multiple workloads onto a single physical host while still isolating them from one another. In traditional IT infrastructures, hardware failure can lead to significant downtime and recovery efforts, as each physical machine operates independently. However, with virtualization, VMs can be moved between physical hosts in the event of a failure, ensuring that workloads are always running on healthy hardware. This flexibility is the basis for many high availability solutions in virtualized environments, as it allows for dynamic resource allocation and recovery in real-time.

VMware vSphere, Microsoft Hyper-V, and other hypervisors offer built-in HA features that automatically detect hardware failures and restart affected VMs on healthy hosts within a cluster. These high availability mechanisms work by leveraging clusters of physical hosts, often referred to as a resource pool, which can work together to provide redundancy and failover capabilities. When a host fails, the VMs running on it are automatically restarted on another host within the same cluster. The hypervisor ensures that the necessary resources are available, whether it involves CPU, memory, or storage, to enable the failover process without requiring manual intervention. The automated recovery process is typically seamless, and in many cases, end users may not even notice that a failure has occurred.

Another important aspect of high availability in virtualized environments is the use of shared storage. For HA to function effectively, the virtual machines must be able to access their data from any host within the cluster. Shared storage solutions, such as Storage Area Networks (SANs) or Network-Attached Storage (NAS), allow multiple hosts to access the same disk storage, making it possible for VMs to be migrated or restarted on different hosts without losing access to their data. Shared storage is also critical for enabling features like live migration, where VMs can be moved between hosts without downtime. The use of shared storage ensures that all VMs within the cluster are synchronized, and it reduces the risk of data loss or inconsistency in the event of a host failure.

In addition to hardware failure recovery, high availability in virtualized environments also involves ensuring that VMs are protected from software failures. Software failures can occur in various forms, including application crashes, operating system failures, or issues related to misconfigured system settings. While HA mechanisms for hardware failures are relatively straightforward, addressing software failures often requires additional measures. For example, administrators can implement monitoring tools to detect abnormal behavior or performance degradation within VMs. These tools can automatically restart VMs or specific applications that are not responding or have crashed. Furthermore, administrators can use backup and disaster recovery solutions that regularly back up the state of the virtual machines to ensure that they can be restored to a previous stable state if software failures occur.

Another technique for achieving high availability in virtualized environments is the use of fault tolerance (FT) mechanisms. Fault tolerance goes beyond traditional HA by providing a continuous, real-time copy of a running VM on another host in the cluster. If the primary VM experiences a failure, the secondary VM immediately takes over without any downtime, providing zero downtime failover. Fault tolerance is particularly valuable in environments where downtime is unacceptable, such as financial institutions, healthcare applications, or any mission-critical systems that require constant uptime. While fault tolerance can be resource-intensive due to the need for duplicate VMs running in parallel, it offers the highest level of availability by ensuring that there is always an exact replica of the VM running in real-time.

Load balancing is another important element of high availability in virtualized environments. It helps prevent a single host from becoming overwhelmed by distributing workloads across multiple hosts within the cluster. By monitoring resource usage across all hosts, load balancing ensures that no single physical machine is overburdened, which could lead to performance degradation or potential failure. In situations where one host is running at full capacity, load balancing can automatically move VMs to other hosts with more available resources, ensuring that each VM performs optimally. This not only prevents downtime but also helps to maintain optimal performance and resource utilization across the entire virtualized infrastructure.

One of the challenges in implementing high availability in virtualized environments is the potential for overcommitment of resources. Virtualization allows for resource overcommitment, where more virtual resources (such as virtual CPUs and memory) are allocated to VMs than are physically available on the host. While this can improve resource utilization, it also increases the risk of performance degradation, especially if too many VMs are running on a single host.

If the host experiences high resource contention or if the number of VMs exceeds the host's capabilities, the performance of the entire environment could be impacted. To address this, administrators must carefully manage resource allocation and monitor the performance of VMs to ensure that overcommitment does not lead to issues with availability.

Another consideration in maintaining high availability is the need for redundancy and network reliability. A failure in the network infrastructure can prevent VMs from communicating with each other or external resources, rendering them unavailable. Ensuring network redundancy through techniques such as network teaming, load balancing, and failover can help mitigate the impact of network failures. In environments that rely heavily on virtualized workloads, it is critical to ensure that the network is just as resilient as the compute and storage resources. Virtual switches and network interfaces must be configured with failover capabilities, ensuring that VMs can continue to communicate even if a network interface goes down.

In addition to network redundancy, administrators should also implement regular testing of high availability mechanisms. Routine failover tests and disaster recovery drills ensure that the HA features are functioning as expected and that recovery procedures are well-practiced. These tests can help identify potential issues with configuration or infrastructure before they affect the operational environment. Testing also provides an opportunity to verify that the failover and recovery processes are seamless and that the VMs can be restored to a working state without causing downtime or data loss.

High availability in virtualized environments requires careful planning, a comprehensive understanding of the infrastructure, and the ability to deploy and manage multiple technologies. While many tools and techniques exist to enable HA, ensuring that all aspects of the environment, from compute and storage to networking, are configured for redundancy and performance is key to maintaining continuous operation. By leveraging features such as live migration, fault tolerance, load balancing, and resource management, administrators can create virtualized environments that offer the highest levels of availability, ensuring that business-critical applications remain operational even in the face of hardware failures, network disruptions, or software issues. High availability not only helps mitigate the risks of downtime but also improves the overall resilience and efficiency of virtualized infrastructures.

Load Balancing for Virtual Machines

Load balancing for virtual machines (VMs) is a vital strategy in managing virtualized environments efficiently. It involves distributing workloads evenly across multiple VMs or physical hosts to ensure that no single VM or host becomes a bottleneck. The goal of load balancing is to optimize resource usage, improve application performance, and ensure high availability by preventing any VM or host from being overwhelmed with too much work. In a virtualized environment, where multiple VMs run on the same physical host, load balancing helps to maintain system stability and ensure that resources are allocated efficiently across the entire infrastructure. By balancing workloads effectively, administrators can maximize the performance and reliability of their virtual machines, reduce downtime, and ensure a smooth end-user experience.

Virtualization introduces a layer of abstraction between the physical hardware and the operating system, allowing for greater flexibility in managing workloads. Since multiple VMs share the same physical host, there is a risk of resource contention if VMs are not balanced properly. Resource contention occurs when one VM consumes too many resources, such as CPU, memory, or storage, which can lead to slow performance or service disruption for other VMs running on the same host. Load balancing mitigates this issue by distributing workloads across hosts, ensuring that resources are utilized efficiently and preventing any single VM from monopolizing critical resources.

One of the primary challenges in virtualized environments is managing resource overcommitment. Overcommitment occurs when the total resources allocated to all VMs exceed the physical resources available on the host. While overcommitting resources can be beneficial in environments where VMs do not use their full resource allocation at all times, it can also lead to performance issues if resources are not managed carefully. Load balancing helps manage overcommitment by dynamically allocating resources based on demand, ensuring that VMs are not competing for the same resources. This can be done by moving VMs from one host to another or adjusting the resource allocation for individual VMs.

In a virtualized infrastructure, load balancing can be achieved through several techniques. One of the most common techniques is vMotion, a feature available in many hypervisors such as VMware vSphere. vMotion allows for the live migration of VMs from one physical host to another without any downtime. This enables administrators to move VMs in response to changing workloads or resource demands, ensuring that resources are distributed more evenly across the hosts. By using vMotion, administrators can prevent resource contention on overloaded hosts, avoid performance degradation, and improve the overall utilization of physical resources.

Another technique for load balancing is resource scheduling. Resource schedulers dynamically allocate CPU, memory, and storage resources to VMs based on their workload requirements. For example, if a VM is running a resource-intensive application, the scheduler may allocate more CPU or memory resources to ensure that the application runs smoothly. Similarly, if a VM is underutilized, the scheduler may reduce its resource allocation, freeing up resources for other VMs that need them more. This dynamic allocation helps to optimize the use of available resources and ensures that VMs are performing at their best.

In addition to CPU and memory, storage is another critical resource that must be balanced in virtualized environments. Storage load balancing ensures that disk I/O is distributed evenly across all available storage devices to prevent any single device from becoming a bottleneck. Virtual storage area networks (vSANs) and other distributed storage solutions can be used to balance storage workloads by spreading data across multiple disks or storage nodes. Storage load balancing ensures that VMs have fast access to the data they need, which is particularly important for applications that rely on high-performance disk I/O, such as databases or virtual desktop infrastructure (VDI) systems.

Network load balancing is equally important in virtualized environments, especially as VMs are often required to communicate with each other and external resources. Network load balancing ensures that network traffic is distributed evenly across multiple network interfaces, preventing any single interface from becoming saturated. This is particularly important in environments with high network throughput demands, such as web hosting, cloud computing, or enterprise applications. By distributing network traffic across multiple interfaces, administrators can ensure that VMs have the bandwidth they need to perform optimally.

Cloud environments, which are typically built on virtualized infrastructures, heavily rely on load balancing to ensure that workloads can scale up or down as needed. In cloud platforms, such as Amazon Web Services (AWS) or Microsoft Azure, load balancing is an integral part of the architecture. Cloud services automatically scale resources based on demand, and load balancing is used to distribute workloads across virtual machines, storage, and network interfaces. This dynamic scaling ensures that resources are always available to meet the demands of users, even during periods of high traffic or increased resource utilization.

In addition to these technical aspects, load balancing also has significant implications for high availability and fault tolerance in virtualized environments. Load balancing ensures that if one VM or host fails, workloads can be moved to other hosts to maintain service continuity. This is particularly important in mission-critical applications where downtime is not acceptable. Load balancing and high availability go hand in hand, as load balancing ensures that resources are distributed evenly, while high availability ensures that if a failure occurs, workloads can quickly be moved to healthy hosts to minimize downtime. This combination of load balancing and high availability helps create a robust and resilient virtualized infrastructure.

For administrators, it is crucial to monitor the performance of the virtualized environment regularly. Monitoring tools can help track resource utilization across hosts and VMs, identify potential bottlenecks, and detect performance degradation before it becomes a major issue. These tools provide insights into CPU, memory, storage, and network usage, allowing administrators to make informed decisions about load balancing and resource allocation. By analyzing historical data and trends, administrators can predict future resource requirements and plan accordingly, ensuring that the virtualized environment can handle increased workloads or scaling demands.

Proper load balancing also helps optimize energy consumption in virtualized data centers. By efficiently distributing workloads across hosts and ensuring that each host is running at optimal capacity, administrators can avoid overloading individual hosts and reduce the energy consumption of underutilized resources. This not only improves the environmental footprint of the data center but also helps reduce operational costs.

Overall, load balancing for virtual machines is an essential practice for managing virtualized environments effectively. It optimizes resource utilization, improves system performance, enhances availability, and ensures that workloads are distributed evenly across the infrastructure. Through techniques such as dynamic resource scheduling, vMotion, and network and storage load balancing, administrators can ensure that virtual machines run efficiently and that the virtualized environment remains scalable and resilient. Effective load balancing helps to create a seamless user experience, reduce downtime, and maintain the stability of virtualized systems, ultimately supporting the demands of modern IT infrastructures.

Virtual Machine Security and Hardening

Virtual machine security and hardening are fundamental aspects of protecting virtualized environments from threats and vulnerabilities. As virtual machines (VMs) become more prevalent in both enterprise and cloud environments, they present unique security challenges. Virtual machines offer flexibility, scalability, and cost savings, but they also introduce risks that need to be managed carefully. A compromised VM can potentially impact the entire virtualized infrastructure, making it essential to ensure that these machines are properly secured and hardened. Virtual machine security involves a multi-layered approach, incorporating measures to protect the VM itself, the hypervisor, and the underlying physical infrastructure. By implementing robust security and hardening techniques, administrators can significantly reduce the risk of attacks and ensure that VMs are resilient against a variety of threats.

The first step in virtual machine security is securing the VM itself. Like physical machines, virtual machines are vulnerable to attacks from malware, unauthorized access, and system vulnerabilities. One of the primary ways to secure a VM is by ensuring that it is running the latest security patches and updates. Just as on physical servers, keeping the operating system (OS) and software up to date is critical in preventing exploitation of known vulnerabilities. Hypervisors, such as VMware ESXi, Microsoft Hyper-V, and others, often provide mechanisms for automatic updates, but it is still important for administrators to verify that all VMs within their environment are regularly patched and free from known vulnerabilities.

In addition to updating the OS and applications, hardening the VM involves minimizing the attack surface by disabling unnecessary services, ports, and software. By default, many operating systems come with features or services that are not needed for the specific role of the VM. Disabling these services reduces the potential points of entry for attackers. For example, if a VM does not require SSH access, the SSH service should be disabled to prevent attackers from attempting to exploit this service. Similarly, unused ports should be closed, and only the necessary ports for the specific application or service should remain open. Removing unnecessary software and features can also prevent vulnerabilities in software that is not being used but may still be a potential target.

Another critical aspect of virtual machine security is the use of strong access controls. As with any other system, it is essential to control who has access to the VM and what they can do once they are inside. Implementing strong authentication mechanisms, such as multi-factor authentication (MFA), is essential to ensure that only authorized personnel can access the VM. In addition, the principle of least privilege should be applied to minimize the permissions granted to users or services. This means that users should only be given the minimum level of access required to perform their job functions, and unnecessary administrative privileges should be avoided. Proper access control mechanisms help prevent unauthorized access to sensitive data and configurations within the VM.

Network security is also an integral part of virtual machine hardening. Since VMs rely on virtual networks to communicate with other systems and external resources, it is important to secure the network interfaces and isolate VMs from unnecessary network access. Using virtual firewalls, network segmentation, and virtual private networks (VPNs) helps ensure that only authorized traffic can reach the VM. Virtualized environments should also take advantage of virtual private networks (VPNs) to encrypt communications between VMs and external systems, preventing eavesdropping and man-in-the-middle attacks. Additionally, configuring virtual switches and network adapters with appropriate security settings ensures that VMs are isolated from each other when necessary, reducing the risk of lateral movement in case one VM is compromised.

While securing the individual VM is important, it is equally critical to secure the underlying hypervisor and the virtualized infrastructure itself. The hypervisor is the software layer responsible for managing the virtual machines, and if it is compromised, an attacker could potentially control all the VMs running on the host. Hypervisor security is paramount in any virtualized environment. One way to protect the hypervisor is by ensuring that it is running on a secure and properly configured host system. Administrators should configure secure boot processes, monitor hypervisor logs for unusual activity, and apply patches to address vulnerabilities as soon as they are discovered. It is also important to implement strong access controls on the hypervisor itself to prevent unauthorized users from gaining access to the management interface.

In addition to securing the hypervisor, securing the host machine that runs the hypervisor is crucial. The host machine is the physical system on which the virtual machines reside, and if it is compromised, attackers can bypass VM-level security. Therefore, hardening the host system by applying security best practices, such as configuring firewalls, using intrusion detection systems, and ensuring that only authorized users have access, is essential. Furthermore, administrators should regularly audit the host system for any security issues and ensure that it adheres to organizational security policies.

Another important component of virtual machine security is the use of encryption. Encrypting the virtual machine's disk and its associated data ensures that even if an attacker gains access to the underlying storage, they will not be able to read the VM's data without the proper decryption key. Many hypervisors offer built-in encryption features for securing virtual disks, and this should be implemented to protect sensitive data stored on VMs. In addition to disk encryption, encrypting network traffic between VMs and external systems helps prevent eavesdropping and data theft during communication. Encryption adds an extra layer of protection, ensuring that even if physical security is compromised, the data remains secure.

Monitoring and auditing are also critical components of VM security. Administrators should continuously monitor VM activity for signs of suspicious behavior or security incidents. Security tools that integrate with hypervisors can provide insights into VM resource usage, login attempts, and other critical activity. Log files should be collected, analyzed, and stored securely, as they can provide valuable forensic data in the event of a security breach. Regular audits of security configurations, permissions, and access logs help ensure that the VM and its associated infrastructure remain secure over time. Automated tools can assist in performing routine security checks and can alert administrators to potential issues before they escalate.

As virtualized environments become more complex and integral to business operations, securing and hardening virtual machines has become an ongoing process. Virtual machines must be protected from the moment they are provisioned through their entire lifecycle. Administrators should continuously apply security best practices, stay informed about new vulnerabilities, and adapt their security measures to address evolving threats. By ensuring that virtual machines are secured and hardened through the implementation of proper access controls, network security, encryption, and continuous monitoring, organizations can protect their virtualized infrastructure from potential attacks and ensure that their critical workloads remain available and secure. Virtual machine security is not a one-time task but a continuous effort to adapt to new challenges and maintain a strong security posture in an increasingly complex digital landscape.

Configuring Virtual Firewalls and Isolation

Configuring virtual firewalls and isolation is an essential aspect of securing virtualized environments. As virtualization becomes more prevalent in modern data centers, ensuring that virtual machines (VMs) are properly isolated and protected from both internal and external threats is critical. Virtual firewalls and network isolation techniques play a significant role in safeguarding the integrity of virtualized infrastructures by controlling traffic flow between VMs, physical hosts, and external networks. These measures help prevent unauthorized access, mitigate security risks, and ensure that sensitive data and applications are protected from potential breaches or attacks.

A virtual firewall functions similarly to a traditional firewall but operates within the virtualized environment to control traffic between virtual machines, the hypervisor, and external networks. Unlike traditional firewalls that are placed at the perimeter of a network, virtual firewalls are typically deployed at the hypervisor or virtual switch level, where they can inspect and control traffic between VMs on the same host or across multiple hosts within a data center. These firewalls act as a barrier, filtering incoming and outgoing traffic based on predefined rules, such as IP addresses, ports, and protocols, to ensure that only authorized communication is allowed. Configuring virtual firewalls allows administrators to enforce strict access controls, monitor traffic for suspicious activity, and prevent unauthorized connections between VMs.

Virtual firewalls offer several advantages in virtualized environments. One of the key benefits is the ability to implement granular security policies at the VM level. Unlike traditional physical firewalls, which typically protect an entire network segment or subnet, virtual firewalls can be configured to protect individual virtual machines. This level of granularity is particularly useful in multi-tenant environments, such as cloud platforms, where VMs belonging to different customers or departments must be isolated from one another. By configuring separate firewall rules for each VM, administrators can ensure that each virtual machine only communicates with the appropriate systems and services, while preventing unauthorized access or lateral movement within the network.

In addition to providing VM-level security, virtual firewalls can also be used to implement micro-segmentation. Micro-segmentation is a security practice that involves dividing a data center or virtual network into smaller, isolated segments, each with its own set of security policies. This approach limits the scope of potential attacks, as even if a vulnerability is exploited in one segment, the attacker is unable to move laterally to other segments within the network. Virtual firewalls enable administrators to create these isolated segments within the virtualized environment by applying specific security rules and controls to each segment. Micro-segmentation significantly enhances the overall security posture of virtualized infrastructures by reducing the attack surface and preventing the spread of threats.

Another important aspect of configuring virtual firewalls is the use of traffic filtering and monitoring. Virtual firewalls not only control traffic flow but also monitor network activity in real time. They can detect unusual patterns, such as spikes in traffic or attempts to access restricted resources, and generate alerts for administrators to investigate. Traffic monitoring is especially important in environments with high traffic volume or where sensitive data is being transmitted. By configuring logging and alerting mechanisms, administrators can quickly identify and respond to potential security incidents, reducing the risk of data breaches or system compromises. Furthermore, virtual firewalls often support intrusion detection and prevention systems (IDS/IPS), which can identify malicious traffic patterns and automatically block or mitigate threats in real time.

Network isolation is another critical component of securing virtual environments. Isolation involves segmenting network traffic in a way that ensures that different VMs or network resources do not interfere with each other. This can be achieved by creating virtual networks or virtual local area networks (VLANs) within the virtualized environment. VLANs allow administrators to group VMs based on their function, security requirements, or business unit, and enforce network isolation between these groups. For example, VMs running sensitive applications, such as financial systems or databases, can be placed in a separate VLAN with stricter security controls, while less critical VMs can be placed in a different VLAN with more relaxed controls. This approach helps prevent unauthorized access to sensitive data and applications while still allowing communication between VMs within the same VLAN as necessary.

In addition to VLANs, another technique for achieving network isolation is the use of virtual switches and network adapters. Virtual switches are software-based devices that connect virtual machines to one another and to external networks. By configuring virtual switches with appropriate security settings, administrators can isolate traffic between different VMs or between VMs and external systems. Virtual switches can be configured to operate in various modes, such as isolated, private, or public, to meet specific security requirements. For instance, in a private network mode, traffic between VMs is restricted to the virtual network and cannot be routed to external networks, while in a public network mode, VMs can communicate with external systems. This flexibility in network configuration ensures that VMs are properly isolated based on their specific security needs.

Network isolation can also be implemented using firewall rules at the virtual switch level. Virtual firewalls can be configured to block or allow traffic between different virtual networks or between VMs and external networks. By setting up appropriate firewall rules, administrators can ensure that VMs in different segments of the network are unable to communicate unless explicitly authorized. This is particularly important in multi-tenant environments, where customers or departments may require strict isolation from one another to prevent unauthorized access or data leakage.

In addition to isolating network traffic, it is important to apply security controls to the management interfaces of virtual machines. These interfaces, which are used to manage and configure VMs, should be protected with strong authentication methods, such as multi-factor authentication (MFA), and encrypted communication channels. Restricting access to management interfaces helps prevent unauthorized users from making changes to VM configurations or accessing sensitive data. Access controls should be implemented at all levels of the virtualized infrastructure, from the hypervisor to the virtual machine, to ensure that only authorized personnel can modify configurations or access critical resources.

Configuring virtual firewalls and isolation is an ongoing process that requires constant monitoring, testing, and updating. As virtualized environments evolve and new threats emerge, administrators must regularly review and adjust firewall rules and isolation settings to ensure that security measures remain effective. Regular security audits and vulnerability assessments should be conducted to identify potential weaknesses and address them before they can be exploited by attackers. Additionally, administrators should stay informed about the latest security best practices and industry standards to ensure that their virtualized environment remains secure over time.

By implementing and maintaining strong virtual firewalls and isolation measures, organizations can significantly enhance the security of their virtualized infrastructures. These measures help protect VMs from both internal and external threats, ensuring that critical applications and data remain secure. As virtualization continues to play an integral role in modern IT environments, configuring virtual firewalls and network isolation will remain essential to achieving robust security and protecting against the growing landscape of cyber threats.

Using Virtual Machines in Cloud Environments

Virtual machines (VMs) have become a cornerstone of cloud computing, enabling organizations to run applications, services, and workloads in a flexible, scalable, and cost-efficient manner. The use of VMs in cloud environments offers numerous advantages, including the ability to quickly provision resources, easily scale infrastructure, and reduce the costs associated with maintaining physical hardware. As more businesses migrate their workloads to the cloud, understanding how to effectively deploy and manage VMs in these environments is critical to ensuring that resources are utilized optimally and that applications run efficiently. Virtual machines in cloud environments provide a high degree of flexibility, as they can be provisioned, modified, and decommissioned on demand, allowing organizations to meet changing business requirements without the constraints of traditional on-premises infrastructure.

One of the primary benefits of using VMs in the cloud is the ability to quickly scale resources up or down based on demand. Cloud platforms, such as Amazon Web Services (AWS), Microsoft Azure, and Google Cloud, provide users with the ability to create and manage virtual machines through a self-service portal. This means that organizations can instantly provision new VMs to accommodate increased workloads, or scale back resources when demand decreases, ensuring that they only pay for what they use. This dynamic scalability is essential in today's fast-paced business environment, where workloads can fluctuate rapidly and unpredictably. By using virtual machines, businesses can avoid overprovisioning or underutilizing physical infrastructure, which often leads to inefficiencies and increased costs.

Another advantage of using VMs in the cloud is the ability to run different operating systems and applications on the same physical hardware. Cloud providers typically offer a wide range of operating systems, from popular distributions of Linux to various versions of Windows Server, allowing organizations to choose the best environment for their applications. This flexibility enables businesses to run a diverse set of applications and services on a single cloud infrastructure, without the need for dedicated physical servers for each different workload. Virtualization abstracts the underlying hardware, allowing multiple VMs to run independently, each with its own operating system and software stack, without interfering with one another.

The cloud also offers enhanced reliability and availability when using virtual machines. Many cloud providers offer high availability features that ensure VMs are resilient to hardware failures or other disruptions. For example, cloud environments typically involve the use of multiple data centers, spread across geographic regions, which are connected by high-speed networks. This geographic distribution of resources enables cloud providers to implement fault tolerance and redundancy, ensuring that VMs can be moved between physical servers or data centers without downtime. In the event of hardware failure, cloud platforms can automatically migrate VMs to healthy hosts, minimizing the impact on the workloads they are running. This ability to quickly recover from failures makes cloud-based VMs a highly reliable option for critical applications that require continuous uptime.

In addition to high availability, security is another critical consideration when using virtual machines in cloud environments. While cloud providers typically implement robust security measures at the infrastructure level, such as encryption, firewalls, and intrusion detection systems, the security of individual VMs must also be managed by the users. Administrators must ensure that each VM is configured with proper access controls, such as strong authentication mechanisms and least-privilege access, to prevent unauthorized access. Furthermore, because VMs can be easily replicated, administrators should ensure that any sensitive data stored on VMs is encrypted both at rest and in transit, preventing exposure if the VM is moved between different cloud regions or environments.

Virtual machines in cloud environments also offer significant advantages in terms of cost efficiency. Traditionally, businesses have had to invest heavily in physical hardware, which comes with costs for procurement, maintenance, and power consumption. In contrast, cloud platforms operate on a pay-as-you-go model, where users are charged based on the resources they consume, such as CPU, memory, storage, and network bandwidth. This model eliminates the need for large upfront investments in hardware and allows businesses to scale their infrastructure based on actual usage. This cost efficiency is particularly beneficial for organizations that experience variable workloads, as they can avoid the expense of maintaining underutilized hardware during periods of low demand.

VMs in the cloud also provide enhanced flexibility for disaster recovery and backup. Cloud platforms offer built-in tools for creating snapshots and backups of virtual machines, which can be used to restore a VM to a previous state in the event of failure or data loss. Cloud-based backups are typically stored in geographically distributed locations, ensuring that data is protected from localized disasters, such as hardware failures, power outages, or natural disasters. In addition, cloud providers often offer features such as automated backup scheduling and disaster recovery solutions, allowing businesses to automate the process of securing their data and ensuring business continuity in the event of a disaster.

Despite the many advantages, there are also challenges when it comes to using VMs in cloud environments. One of the main concerns is the complexity of managing and orchestrating multiple VMs across different cloud platforms or within a hybrid environment. As organizations move to multi-cloud or hybrid cloud models, managing VMs in these distributed environments can become increasingly complex. To address this, cloud providers offer orchestration tools and platforms that help automate the provisioning, monitoring, and management of virtual machines across multiple environments. These tools can help streamline operations, reduce manual intervention, and ensure consistency in the configuration and deployment of VMs.

Another challenge in cloud-based virtual machine management is the need to optimize resource utilization. In cloud environments, users may quickly spin up multiple VMs to meet demand, but inefficient resource allocation can lead to wasted resources and higher costs. Administrators must ensure that VMs are appropriately sized for their workloads and that resource allocation is adjusted dynamically based on performance metrics. Many cloud platforms offer auto-scaling features, where VMs are automatically resized or added based on demand, but administrators must carefully monitor usage patterns to ensure that auto-scaling is configured correctly and that resources are not overcommitted.

VMs in cloud environments also introduce new considerations regarding network performance. While cloud providers offer high-speed networking between VMs and other cloud resources, network latency and bandwidth can still impact the performance of cloud-based applications. Administrators must carefully plan network configurations to ensure that VMs can communicate efficiently with each other and with external systems. Virtual networks, load balancing, and content delivery networks (CDNs) are often used in cloud environments to optimize network performance and ensure that applications are responsive and performant.

Using virtual machines in cloud environments provides organizations with significant flexibility, scalability, and cost savings. The ability to quickly provision, scale, and manage VMs allows businesses to meet the demands of a dynamic and evolving IT landscape. With cloud-based VMs, businesses can run a wide range of applications, from development and testing environments to production workloads, without the need for physical hardware. While there are challenges in managing and optimizing VMs in the cloud, the benefits of cost efficiency, high availability, and disaster recovery make cloud-based virtual machines a powerful tool for modern organizations.

Virtualization in Data Centers

Virtualization has become a transformative technology in modern data centers, providing a flexible and efficient way to manage IT resources. By abstracting physical hardware resources and creating virtual instances of servers, storage, and networks, virtualization enables organizations to optimize their data center operations, improve scalability, and reduce costs. In traditional data centers, physical servers were dedicated to specific tasks, often resulting in underutilization of resources. Virtualization addresses this inefficiency by allowing multiple virtual machines (VMs) to run on a single physical server, each with its own operating system and application stack. This consolidation of resources leads to significant improvements in resource utilization, flexibility, and operational efficiency.

One of the primary advantages of virtualization in data centers is the ability to increase server consolidation. In a non-virtualized environment, each physical server runs a single operating system instance, often leading to underutilization of hardware resources such as CPU, memory, and storage. By virtualizing these physical servers, multiple virtual machines can be run on a single physical server, allowing organizations to maximize their hardware usage. For example, instead of running one application on a dedicated physical server, virtualization allows several applications to run in isolated VMs on the same server. This consolidation reduces the number of physical servers needed, which in turn lowers hardware, power, and cooling costs. The efficient use of physical resources not only reduces capital expenditures but also minimizes ongoing operational costs.

Another key benefit of virtualization in data centers is improved scalability and flexibility. With traditional physical servers, scaling up or down to meet changing business needs often involves the time-consuming process of purchasing, installing, and configuring new hardware. In contrast, virtualization allows for the rapid provisioning of new virtual machines as needed. Administrators can quickly allocate additional resources, such as CPU, memory, or storage, to existing VMs or deploy new VMs to meet growing demand. This ability to scale resources dynamically ensures that data centers can adapt to fluctuating workloads and evolving business requirements without the delays and expenses associated with procuring new physical hardware.

In addition to scalability, virtualization also enhances flexibility in data center management. Virtual machines can be moved between physical hosts without downtime, a process known as live migration. This capability enables administrators to balance workloads across physical servers, ensuring that no single server becomes overburdened while others remain underutilized. Live migration also plays a crucial role in disaster recovery and maintenance activities. For instance, if a server requires maintenance or fails, VMs can be quickly migrated to another host, minimizing service disruptions and maintaining business continuity. This flexibility is particularly valuable in modern data centers, where uptime and availability are critical to business operations.

Virtualization in data centers also simplifies management and automation. Many virtualization platforms provide centralized management consoles that allow administrators to monitor, configure, and manage all VMs and physical hosts from a single interface. These platforms often include automated provisioning tools that streamline the deployment of new VMs, reducing the time and effort required to bring new systems online. Automation also plays a significant role in optimizing resource allocation. For example, dynamic resource scheduling can automatically allocate resources based on workload demands, ensuring that VMs receive the necessary CPU, memory, and storage resources at all times. This automation reduces the manual intervention required to manage resources, freeing up administrators to focus on more strategic tasks.

One of the most significant benefits of virtualization is the increased efficiency of disaster recovery and backup processes. In a traditional physical data center, disaster recovery often requires replicating entire physical servers, which can be time-consuming and costly. Virtualization simplifies disaster recovery by enabling the creation of VM snapshots, which are essentially point-in-time copies of the virtual machine's state, including its operating system, applications, and data. These snapshots can be used to quickly restore VMs to a previous state in the event of a failure, reducing recovery time and minimizing data loss. Furthermore, virtualization platforms often include features like high availability and automated failover, ensuring that workloads can be quickly moved to healthy hosts in the event of hardware failure. This level of resilience and recovery capability enhances the overall reliability of the data center and reduces the risk of downtime.

Security is another important aspect of virtualization in data centers. Virtualization provides a level of isolation between VMs, ensuring that each VM operates independently of the others, even when running on the same physical host. This isolation can enhance security by preventing unauthorized access to data and applications running in different VMs. For example, if one VM becomes compromised due to a vulnerability or attack, the attacker is limited to that specific VM and cannot easily spread to other VMs running on the same host. Additionally, virtualization platforms often provide advanced security features, such as encryption, access controls, and intrusion detection, that help protect data and applications from unauthorized access or malicious activity.

Despite the many benefits of virtualization, it also presents certain challenges in data center environments. One of the primary concerns is the increased complexity of managing virtualized infrastructure. As more VMs are created and managed within the data center, it becomes more difficult to keep track of resources, configurations, and performance. Without proper management tools and processes, administrators may struggle to ensure that VMs are allocated appropriate resources, that performance is optimized, and that security policies are consistently applied. To address this, organizations must invest in robust management and monitoring tools that can provide visibility into the virtualized infrastructure and ensure that resources are being used efficiently and securely.

Another challenge is the potential for resource contention. In a virtualized environment, multiple VMs share the same physical hardware, which means that resources like CPU, memory, and storage can become oversubscribed if not carefully managed. Resource contention can lead to performance degradation, especially if VMs are not allocated sufficient resources or if too many VMs are running on a single host. To mitigate this risk, administrators must carefully monitor resource usage and implement load balancing and resource scheduling techniques that ensure that VMs receive the necessary resources to function optimally. Additionally, overcommitment of resources must be carefully managed to avoid performance bottlenecks.

Virtualization in data centers also requires careful planning and design to ensure that the underlying hardware and network infrastructure can support the demands of the virtualized environment. As the number of VMs increases, so does the need for high-performance storage, networking, and compute resources. Organizations must ensure that their infrastructure is capable of handling the increased workload and that the network is properly segmented to ensure optimal performance and security. Network performance is particularly critical in virtualized environments, where multiple VMs may need to communicate with each other and with external systems. Ensuring that the network can support the traffic load generated by VMs is essential for maintaining performance and minimizing latency.

The use of virtualization in data centers has revolutionized the way organizations manage and deploy IT resources. By enabling the consolidation of physical servers, improving scalability, and enhancing disaster recovery capabilities, virtualization has become an indispensable tool in modern data centers. However, to fully realize the benefits of virtualization, organizations must carefully manage and monitor their virtualized environments, ensuring that resources are properly allocated, security is maintained, and performance is optimized. As virtualization technology continues to evolve, its role in data centers will only become more critical, enabling organizations to meet the demands of increasingly complex and dynamic workloads.

Cost Considerations in Virtual Machine Management

Managing virtual machines (VMs) in a modern IT infrastructure can bring significant benefits, including increased flexibility, scalability, and resource optimization. However, as with any technology, the management of VMs introduces various cost considerations that must be carefully evaluated to ensure that the organization maximizes the benefits of virtualization while minimizing expenses. These costs are not only financial but also operational and strategic. Virtual machine management can have both direct and indirect costs, and organizations must be proactive in understanding these factors to make informed decisions that align with their business goals.

One of the most immediate costs associated with virtual machine management is the infrastructure cost. Virtualization relies on physical hardware to host multiple virtual machines, and this infrastructure must be robust enough to support the required workloads. While virtualization enables the consolidation of physical servers, which reduces the number of machines required, the underlying hardware still needs to be high-performance and capable of handling the resource demands of numerous VMs. Overcommitting resources, such as CPU, memory, or storage, can lead to resource contention, performance issues, and ultimately, more expense to resolve these issues. As such, investing in high-quality servers, networking, and storage systems is necessary to ensure that the virtualized environment operates efficiently without excessive hardware failures or bottlenecks.

In addition to the initial capital expenditure on hardware, ongoing maintenance costs must also be considered. Servers, storage systems, and networking components require regular maintenance and occasional upgrades to remain operational and secure. These maintenance costs include patching, monitoring, troubleshooting, and replacing hardware as needed. As the number of VMs increases, the complexity of the infrastructure also grows, requiring more frequent attention and more sophisticated management tools. This can lead to increased labor costs for IT staff who need to monitor the health of the environment, manage resource allocation, and ensure that the VMs and the underlying hardware continue to perform optimally.

Another important cost consideration is energy consumption. Although virtualization can improve resource utilization by consolidating workloads onto fewer physical servers, it does not eliminate the need for power. In fact, in some cases, it may increase energy use due to the need for more powerful servers or more sophisticated cooling systems to handle the concentrated workloads of multiple VMs. Data centers, especially those running large-scale virtualized infrastructures, can incur substantial electricity costs for both running servers and cooling them. Organizations must balance the benefits of virtualization with the operational costs of powering and cooling the infrastructure to ensure that the total cost of ownership remains manageable.

Storage is another significant cost factor in virtual machine management. Virtual machines require storage for their operating systems, applications, and data, and in virtualized environments, storage must be allocated efficiently to avoid both underutilization and overuse. In many cases, organizations opt for shared storage systems, such as Storage Area Networks (SANs) or Network-Attached Storage (NAS), to ensure that VMs can be easily migrated between hosts and that data is accessible from multiple locations. While shared storage provides flexibility, it can also be expensive, especially in high-performance configurations. Virtual machines can also generate large amounts of data, especially in environments with heavy workloads, requiring additional storage resources to accommodate growth. This can result in the need for higher-capacity storage devices or services, increasing both upfront and operational costs.

Licensing is another often overlooked but critical cost consideration in virtual machine management. Virtualization requires not only licenses for the hypervisor software but also additional licenses for the operating systems and applications that run on virtual machines. In some cases, software vendors charge for licenses based on the number of VMs or the amount of allocated CPU or memory, which can increase costs as the number of VMs scales. Licensing models can be complex, and organizations must be diligent in tracking the number of VMs and ensuring that they remain compliant with licensing agreements. Failure to properly manage licensing can lead to unexpected costs in the form of fines or penalties, or even the need to purchase additional licenses when scaling the environment.

Management tools and software for virtualized environments also represent a significant cost. While hypervisor platforms like VMware vSphere, Microsoft Hyper-V, and others come with basic management capabilities, most organizations require additional tools for monitoring, resource management, backup, disaster recovery, and security. These tools help administrators ensure that VMs are performing optimally, that resources are allocated effectively, and that the environment is secure. However, many of these management tools come at an additional cost, whether through licensing fees, subscriptions, or professional services. The complexity of managing large-scale virtualized environments often requires investing in advanced tools to ensure that the environment remains secure, efficient, and easy to manage. These tools are essential to maintaining the performance and security of the virtualized infrastructure but contribute to the overall cost of virtual machine management.

Operational overhead is another indirect cost associated with virtual machine management. While virtualization can reduce hardware costs and improve resource utilization, the complexity of managing numerous virtual machines and the associated infrastructure can increase the operational burden. IT staff must regularly monitor VM performance, manage resources, apply patches and updates, troubleshoot issues, and handle security concerns. As the number of VMs increases, so too does the complexity of managing these systems, requiring more skilled personnel or additional training for existing staff. Additionally, larger virtualized environments often require more robust backup and disaster recovery solutions to ensure that data can be restored in the event of a failure. These operational tasks can quickly add up in terms of both time and labor costs.

Security is another critical consideration in the cost of managing virtual machines. With virtualized environments, the attack surface increases because multiple VMs share the same physical infrastructure. This necessitates a greater investment in security measures to protect both the VMs and the underlying hardware. Virtual machine security involves patch management, intrusion detection systems, firewalls, encryption, and the proper configuration of access controls. The complexity of securing a virtualized environment often leads organizations to invest in specialized security solutions, increasing the overall cost of managing virtual machines. Furthermore, with the growing prevalence of cyber threats, organizations must continually update their security strategies to address emerging risks, leading to an ongoing financial commitment.

While virtualization in data centers offers significant benefits in terms of cost savings, resource optimization, and scalability, there are a variety of costs associated with managing virtual machines that organizations must consider. From infrastructure investments and operational costs to licensing, storage, and security measures, the total cost of managing VMs can add up quickly. By carefully managing resources, optimizing infrastructure, and selecting the right tools for the job, organizations can mitigate these costs while reaping the benefits of virtualization. However, this requires ongoing monitoring, planning, and decision-making to ensure that virtual machine management remains cost-effective and aligned with the organization's broader business goals.

Virtual Machine Automation with Scripts

Virtual machine (VM) automation is a powerful tool that enhances the efficiency and flexibility of managing virtualized environments. Through the use of scripts, administrators can automate routine tasks such as provisioning, configuring, monitoring, and managing virtual machines. Scripting provides a way to streamline repetitive processes, reduce human error, and ensure consistency across large-scale virtual environments. Virtual machine automation is especially critical in cloud computing and large data centers where the number of VMs can grow exponentially. With scripts, IT professionals can efficiently scale, maintain, and manage VMs without the need for manual intervention, saving time and resources while ensuring a more reliable infrastructure.

One of the most common use cases for virtual machine automation is the provisioning of new VMs. In a traditional setup, provisioning a VM manually can be time-consuming, requiring the administrator to configure the operating system, install necessary software, and apply specific settings. Automation through scripts can significantly reduce the time it takes to deploy a new VM by creating predefined templates for each type of VM and applying those templates automatically. Scripts can handle everything from creating the VM, configuring networking, and applying operating system settings, to installing required applications. This not only saves time but also ensures that all VMs are provisioned consistently, adhering to organizational standards. Automated provisioning can be particularly beneficial in cloud environments, where scaling up or down quickly is essential to meet changing business demands.

Another area where scripting and automation shine is in the management of VM configurations. Once a VM is provisioned, administrators must ensure that it is configured properly, including assigning CPU and memory resources, configuring network interfaces, and managing storage. Automating these configuration tasks using scripts can help eliminate inconsistencies and ensure that each VM is configured according to best practices. For example, a script can be written to ensure that all newly provisioned VMs receive the appropriate amount of CPU and memory allocation, configure specific network settings, and install the necessary software packages. By using automation to configure VMs, administrators can ensure that their virtual environments are optimized for performance and security while minimizing the risk of human error.

Monitoring is another essential task that can benefit from virtual machine automation. In a large virtualized environment, keeping track of the health and performance of all VMs can become increasingly difficult. Manually checking the status of each VM, monitoring resource usage, and identifying issues such as performance degradation or resource contention can be a tedious and error-prone process. With automation scripts, administrators can create scheduled tasks to monitor the status of VMs, check resource utilization, and generate alerts if any VMs are underperforming or experiencing issues. These scripts can be configured to monitor key performance metrics such as CPU usage, memory consumption, disk I/O, and network traffic. By automating the monitoring process, administrators can proactively identify and address issues before they impact the operation of the virtualized environment.

Automation also plays a key role in patch management and software updates for virtual machines. Keeping VMs up to date with the latest patches and security updates is critical for maintaining the integrity and security of the environment. However, manually updating each VM can be time-consuming, especially in large-scale environments. Scripts can automate the patch management process by checking for updates, downloading and installing patches, and rebooting VMs as necessary. By scheduling these tasks to run at specific intervals or during off-peak hours, administrators can ensure that VMs are always up to date without disrupting operations. Automation also ensures that patches are applied consistently across all VMs, reducing the risk of vulnerabilities caused by missing updates.

In addition to routine maintenance, automation with scripts can assist with backup and disaster recovery processes. Regularly backing up virtual machines is essential to protect against data loss, especially in production environments. Scripts can be written to automate the backup process, ensuring that VMs are regularly backed up according to a defined schedule. These scripts can automate tasks such as creating snapshots of VMs, copying VM data to remote storage, and verifying the integrity of backups. In the event of a failure, automated disaster recovery scripts can be used to restore VMs from backups, ensuring minimal downtime and data loss. By automating the backup and recovery process, organizations can implement a more reliable and efficient disaster recovery strategy.

Virtual machine automation with scripts also simplifies tasks such as scaling virtual environments. As demand for resources fluctuates, administrators may need to add or remove VMs to match the load. Manually creating and configuring new VMs or decommissioning old ones can be time-consuming and inefficient. With automation, scripts can be used to automatically provision new VMs when resource utilization reaches a certain threshold or automatically shut down and delete unused VMs to free up resources. By automating the scaling process, organizations can ensure that their virtualized environment is always optimally configured to meet demand without over-provisioning or underutilizing resources.

Security is another area where virtual machine automation can provide significant benefits. Virtual machines must be configured with strict security measures to protect sensitive data and prevent unauthorized access. Scripts can be used to automate security tasks such as configuring firewalls, setting up user accounts and permissions, and applying security patches. Additionally, automation can be used to ensure that security policies are consistently applied across all VMs, reducing the risk of misconfiguration or human error. For example, a script could be used to ensure that all VMs have up-to-date antivirus software installed and that firewalls are configured correctly to restrict unauthorized access.

Despite the numerous advantages of automating virtual machine management, it is important to be mindful of potential challenges. One such challenge is ensuring that the automation scripts are correctly written and tested. Poorly designed scripts can cause unintended consequences, such as misconfiguring VMs or inadvertently interrupting critical services. To mitigate this risk, administrators should test automation scripts in a controlled environment before deploying them to production systems. Additionally, version control and documentation are essential for managing and maintaining scripts over time. As virtual environments evolve and new tasks are added, scripts must be updated and maintained to ensure they remain effective and accurate.

Furthermore, as virtual environments become more complex, the management of automation scripts can become increasingly difficult. For large-scale environments, administrators may need to implement orchestration tools that allow them to manage and coordinate the execution of multiple scripts across different systems and platforms. These orchestration tools provide a centralized interface for managing automation workflows, making it easier to automate complex processes and integrate multiple systems. While automation offers significant benefits, it requires careful planning and oversight to ensure that the virtual machine management process remains efficient, secure, and error-free.

Virtual machine automation with scripts is a powerful tool for managing and optimizing virtualized environments. By automating tasks such as provisioning, configuration, monitoring, patch management, backup, and scaling, organizations can improve efficiency, reduce human error, and ensure consistency across their infrastructure. Automation also enables organizations to respond more quickly to changing business needs, optimize resource utilization, and implement a more effective disaster recovery strategy. However, careful planning, testing, and ongoing maintenance are necessary to ensure that automation scripts are effective and do not introduce unintended risks. With the right approach, virtual machine automation can significantly enhance the management of virtualized environments, leading to more reliable, scalable, and cost-effective IT operations.

Integrating Virtualization with Other IT Systems

Integrating virtualization with other IT systems is a crucial aspect of modern enterprise architecture, as it enables organizations to leverage the full potential of their IT infrastructure. Virtualization itself provides a level of abstraction that allows for the efficient use of physical hardware, but to realize its full benefits, it must be seamlessly integrated with other systems such as storage, networking, monitoring, backup, and security. Effective integration of these components with virtualized environments enhances scalability, improves performance, ensures resilience, and simplifies management. This integration allows businesses to create a cohesive, flexible, and highly efficient IT ecosystem that can respond dynamically to changing business requirements.

One of the key areas of integration in virtualized environments is storage. Virtualization typically relies on shared storage systems such as Storage Area Networks (SANs) or Network-Attached Storage (NAS) to provide access to data for virtual machines (VMs). These storage solutions need to be integrated with the virtualization platform to ensure seamless access to virtual disks and data across all hosts in a virtualized cluster. The integration between storage and virtualization platforms allows for the easy migration of VMs between hosts, centralized management of storage resources, and the ability to allocate storage dynamically to VMs as needed. Furthermore, shared storage is critical for implementing high availability and disaster recovery features, such as VM failover and live migration. Storage systems that are tightly integrated with virtualization platforms enable administrators to optimize storage performance, reduce costs, and ensure that data is always available, even in the event of a host failure.

Networking is another vital component that must be effectively integrated with virtualization. Virtual networks allow VMs to communicate with each other and external systems, and managing network traffic in a virtualized environment requires careful configuration and integration with the underlying physical network infrastructure. Virtualized environments often involve complex network setups, such as virtual switches, network adapters, and VLANs (Virtual Local Area Networks), which need to be configured to ensure that VMs can communicate securely and efficiently. Integrating the virtualization platform with network management tools allows administrators to configure, monitor, and control network traffic between VMs and across different hosts. This integration is essential for optimizing network performance, ensuring security, and maintaining proper network segmentation. With the right integration, administrators can implement features like load balancing, network isolation, and high availability, all of which improve the reliability and performance of the network in virtualized environments.

Security is another area where virtualization integration is crucial. Virtualized environments introduce additional security challenges because multiple VMs share the same physical hardware, increasing the risk of cross-VM attacks if proper isolation and security measures are not in place. Integrating virtualization with security systems such as firewalls, intrusion detection/prevention systems (IDS/IPS), and security information and event management (SIEM) tools helps ensure that VMs are protected from external and internal threats. For example, security policies can be applied to virtual networks to control traffic between VMs and external systems, while security tools can monitor VM activity for signs of unusual behavior. Integration with identity and access management (IAM) systems ensures that only authorized users have access to the virtualized infrastructure and can make changes to VMs or their configurations. Security integration with virtualization ensures that VMs are protected from attacks, and data is kept secure, even in multi-tenant environments where VMs from different customers or departments coexist on the same physical infrastructure.

Backup and disaster recovery systems must also be tightly integrated with virtualized environments to ensure that data and applications are protected. Virtual machines, by their very nature, are highly mobile and dynamic, and their state can change rapidly as resources are allocated, deallocated, and migrated between hosts. Backup systems that are not integrated with virtualization platforms may struggle to keep up with these changes, leading to inconsistent backups or difficulty restoring VMs after a failure. When backup solutions are integrated with virtualization, they can capture snapshots of VMs, which represent the state of the entire system, including the operating system, applications, and data. These snapshots can be scheduled to run at regular intervals and can be used for quick recovery in the event of system failure or data loss. Additionally, disaster recovery plans that are integrated with virtualized environments enable automated failover, where VMs can be quickly moved to healthy hosts in the event of a failure, ensuring minimal downtime and business continuity.

Monitoring is another critical component that requires integration with virtualization platforms to provide real-time insights into the health, performance, and utilization of the virtualized environment. Virtualization management platforms often provide basic monitoring capabilities, but integrating these platforms with more advanced monitoring and analytics tools allows for a deeper understanding of the infrastructure's performance. Monitoring tools can track metrics such as CPU and memory utilization, disk I/O, network traffic, and VM uptime, alerting administrators to potential issues before they escalate. By integrating monitoring tools with automation and orchestration platforms, administrators can set thresholds for resource usage, enabling automated responses such as adjusting resources, moving VMs, or triggering alerts. Effective monitoring integration helps ensure that the virtualized infrastructure remains healthy, performs optimally, and can quickly adapt to changing workload demands.

Automation and orchestration are critical aspects of managing virtualized environments, particularly as the number of VMs grows. By integrating virtualization platforms with automation tools, administrators can streamline tasks such as provisioning, scaling, patching, and configuration management. Automation can be used to automatically deploy new VMs, allocate resources, and apply patches, reducing the need for manual intervention and improving consistency.

Orchestration tools allow administrators to define workflows that can automatically scale infrastructure based on demand, move VMs between hosts for load balancing, or implement disaster recovery procedures. The integration of virtualization with automation and orchestration platforms helps organizations manage large, dynamic environments more efficiently and respond quickly to changing business requirements.

The integration of virtualization with cloud platforms is another area that enhances the scalability and flexibility of virtualized environments. Many organizations use hybrid cloud architectures, where on-premises virtualized resources are integrated with public or private cloud platforms to provide a seamless extension of infrastructure. This integration allows workloads to be moved between on-premises data centers and the cloud based on demand, providing additional capacity and ensuring business continuity. Cloud platforms provide elastic resources that can scale up or down automatically, and when combined with virtualization, they enable organizations to optimize their IT infrastructure for both cost efficiency and performance. Integration with cloud platforms also enables disaster recovery capabilities, where cloud resources can be used as a backup in the event of a failure in the on-premises infrastructure.

Finally, IT service management (ITSM) systems can be integrated with virtualization platforms to enhance the overall management and delivery of IT services. By integrating virtualization with ITSM tools, organizations can automate the creation, management, and tracking of service requests related to virtual machines. For example, when a user requests a new VM, the ITSM system can trigger an automated workflow that provisions the VM, configures the necessary resources, and notifies the user when the VM is ready. Integration with ITSM tools helps streamline IT operations, improve service delivery, and enhance visibility into the performance and availability of virtualized resources.

Integrating virtualization with other IT systems is crucial for creating a cohesive, efficient, and scalable IT environment. By connecting virtualization platforms with storage, networking, security, backup, monitoring, and other systems, organizations can ensure that their virtualized infrastructure is optimized for performance, availability, and security. Integration allows for the seamless management of complex virtual environments, enabling businesses to respond quickly to changing demands, scale resources as needed, and maintain a reliable and resilient IT infrastructure. As organizations continue to adopt virtualization and cloud technologies, the importance of integration will only grow, making it a key component of modern IT strategy.

Virtual Machine Backup and Data Protection

Virtual machine (VM) backup and data protection are essential components of modern IT infrastructure management. As organizations continue to rely on virtualized environments to run critical applications and store sensitive data, the need for robust backup strategies becomes more apparent. Virtual machines provide flexibility and scalability, allowing businesses to efficiently allocate resources and manage workloads. However, with this flexibility comes the responsibility of ensuring that VMs are protected from data loss, system failures, and other disasters. A well-designed backup strategy not only safeguards virtual machines but also ensures business continuity and enables rapid recovery in the event of a failure.

Backup solutions for virtual machines differ significantly from traditional physical machine backup approaches due to the unique nature of virtualization. Unlike physical servers, which are discrete entities with dedicated hardware resources, virtual machines are software-defined and share the underlying hardware of a host system. This means that VM backups must take into account both the state of the virtual machine itself and its associated storage, network configurations, and virtualized resources. Virtual machine backup solutions must therefore be capable of capturing the entire state of the VM, including the operating system, applications, and data, to allow for a complete and consistent recovery.

The process of backing up virtual machines begins with selecting the appropriate backup solution. There are several types of backup techniques used in virtualized environments, including image-based backups, file-level backups, and application-aware backups. Image-based backups capture the entire state of the VM, including the operating system, configuration, applications, and data, in a single snapshot. This type of backup is particularly useful for disaster recovery scenarios, as it allows the VM to be restored quickly to its previous state. Image-based backups are often used in conjunction with other backup methods to ensure comprehensive protection, as they capture a complete image of the VM at a specific point in time.

File-level backups, on the other hand, focus on backing up individual files and directories within a virtual machine. This method is often used for backing up specific data or files that are critical to the organization's operations. While file-level backups are not as comprehensive as image-based backups, they can be useful for situations where only specific files need to be restored or when performing regular incremental backups. Application-aware backups take this a step further by ensuring that backup solutions are aware of the applications running on the virtual machine. This approach is particularly important for databases, email servers, and other mission-critical applications, as it ensures that the backup captures the data in a consistent state, preventing issues with data corruption during restoration.

The frequency of VM backups is another key consideration. While full backups are necessary for disaster recovery, they can be time-consuming and resource-intensive. As a result, many organizations adopt a strategy that combines full backups with incremental or differential backups. Incremental backups capture only the changes made since the last backup, reducing the amount of data that needs to be stored and speeding up the backup process. Differential backups, on the other hand, capture changes made since the last full backup. These approaches allow organizations to balance backup frequency and storage requirements while ensuring that data is adequately protected.

In addition to backup frequency, the location of backups is a critical factor in virtual machine data protection. Storing backups locally on the same physical infrastructure as the VMs can be convenient but poses risks in the event of a hardware failure or disaster. A more robust approach is to store backups offsite, either in remote data centers or cloud storage, to protect against localized disasters such as fires, floods, or power outages. Cloud-based backup solutions offer scalability, flexibility, and offsite storage, making them an increasingly popular choice for VM data protection. Cloud storage also provides the added benefit of enabling easy access to backups from anywhere, facilitating remote recovery and reducing the risk of data loss.

Data deduplication is another important factor in virtual machine backup strategies. Virtualized environments often involve the use of many similar or identical VMs, which can result in redundancy in the backup data. Data deduplication is a technique that eliminates this redundancy by identifying and removing duplicate data during the backup process. This reduces the amount of storage required for backups and can significantly lower the cost of maintaining backup systems. Deduplication is particularly effective in environments where multiple VMs share similar configurations or operating systems.

Virtual machine backup solutions should also integrate with disaster recovery (DR) plans. In the event of a failure, it is essential to have a well-defined process for restoring VMs and ensuring that business operations can continue with minimal disruption. Many backup solutions for VMs offer built-in disaster recovery features, such as automated failover, replication, and VM migration. These features ensure that if a VM fails or a host becomes unavailable, workloads can be quickly moved to another host or replicated to a secondary site. Automated recovery processes help reduce downtime and minimize the impact on users and applications. Additionally, the integration of VM backup solutions with broader IT service management systems ensures that recovery procedures are well-documented, tested, and rehearsed.

Backup verification is another important aspect of virtual machine data protection. It is not enough to simply perform backups; organizations must regularly test and verify the integrity of their backups to ensure they are recoverable in the event of a failure. This includes checking that the backup process completed successfully, verifying the consistency of the backup data, and performing test restores to ensure that VMs can be brought back online quickly. Backup verification should be an ongoing practice, and organizations should implement regular testing schedules to ensure that their backup systems remain effective over time.

Security is also a critical consideration in virtual machine backup strategies. Backups contain sensitive data, and unauthorized access to backup files can result in data breaches, loss of intellectual property, or regulatory compliance violations. Encryption should be applied to backup data to ensure that it remains protected both at rest and in transit. Access controls should be implemented to restrict backup data access to authorized personnel only, and backup solutions should include features such as multi-factor authentication and audit logs to monitor and track access to backup systems.

The management of backup storage is another important consideration for virtual machine data protection. As the volume of data grows, organizations need to consider how to store, organize, and retrieve backup data efficiently. Long-term retention policies should be defined to determine how long backups are kept and when they are archived or deleted. Backup solutions should support flexible storage options, allowing organizations to store backups on disk, tape, or cloud storage based on their specific needs and budget.

Virtual machine backup and data protection are integral parts of a comprehensive IT strategy. By implementing the right backup solutions, organizations can safeguard their virtualized infrastructure against data loss, hardware failures, and other disasters. Whether through image-based, file-level, or application-aware backups, the goal is to ensure that data is protected, recoverable, and available when needed most. Proper backup strategies, coupled with disaster recovery integration, automation, and security measures, enable organizations to maintain business continuity and mitigate risks in an increasingly complex virtualized world.

Disaster Recovery Planning with Virtual Machines

Disaster recovery planning is a critical component of any IT strategy, and with the growing reliance on virtualized infrastructures, it is essential to adapt recovery strategies to support virtual machines (VMs). Virtual machines offer many advantages, including flexibility, scalability, and resource optimization, but they also introduce new challenges when it comes to disaster recovery (DR). Effective disaster recovery planning with virtual machines involves ensuring that virtualized environments are protected, data is backed up, and systems can be quickly restored in the event of an unexpected failure. This planning includes considering how to recover both individual VMs and the entire virtualized infrastructure to minimize downtime and data loss while ensuring business continuity.

One of the first considerations in disaster recovery planning for virtual machines is the creation of a robust backup strategy. Virtual machines, like physical systems, are susceptible to data loss due to hardware failures, software malfunctions, or human error. Having an effective backup system in place is essential for ensuring that VM data can be restored when needed. Image-based backups, which capture the entire state of a VM—including its operating system, applications, and data—are commonly used for virtualized environments. These backups enable the recovery of the entire virtual machine in the event of a failure, ensuring that no data is lost and that the VM can be restored to its original state. Backup frequency is another key consideration; regular and incremental backups help minimize data loss between full backup cycles, enabling organizations to restore VMs to the most recent point of operational functionality.

In addition to backup strategies, disaster recovery planning with virtual machines must also account for high availability (HA) configurations. High availability ensures that VMs remain operational even if a physical host or individual VM fails. In virtualized environments, this can be achieved by leveraging features like live migration and VM failover. Live migration allows VMs to be moved from one physical host to another without downtime, ensuring that workloads can continue to run without interruption. VM failover ensures that in the event of a failure, VMs can be automatically restarted on another host in a cluster, reducing downtime and maintaining business continuity. These HA features can be crucial in minimizing service disruption during disasters and ensuring that critical applications remain available to users.

Another critical element in disaster recovery planning for virtual machines is the use of replication. Replication involves creating and maintaining copies of VMs or virtual disks in remote locations. In the event of a disaster at the primary data center, replicated VMs can be quickly brought online in a secondary location, ensuring that business operations can continue with minimal interruption. There are various methods of VM replication, such as synchronous and asynchronous replication. Synchronous replication ensures that data is replicated in real-time, providing near-zero data loss, while asynchronous replication has a slight delay between the primary and secondary locations but can be more bandwidth-efficient. Depending on the organization's needs, replication can be set up to protect individual VMs, entire clusters, or even storage arrays. Replication allows organizations to safeguard against data loss caused by hardware failures, natural disasters, or regional outages.

Failover and replication strategies are often complemented by disaster recovery orchestration. Orchestration tools automate and streamline the recovery process by defining and executing recovery workflows. These tools ensure that recovery steps are executed in the correct sequence, minimizing human intervention and reducing recovery time. Orchestration tools can automatically deploy VMs, configure network settings, restore data, and bring applications back online according to predefined recovery plans. This level of automation is essential in large-scale environments where manually recovering VMs can be time-consuming and error-prone. Additionally, disaster recovery orchestration can provide real-time visibility into the status of recovery operations, allowing administrators to track progress and intervene if necessary.

In virtualized environments, network connectivity plays a crucial role in disaster recovery planning. When VMs are recovered or migrated to a secondary site, it is essential that they are properly connected to the network to ensure that users and applications can continue to operate seamlessly. Network configuration should be part of the disaster recovery plan, ensuring that virtual networks, virtual switches, and other network components are replicated and configured correctly in the secondary site. This includes ensuring that IP addresses, VLAN configurations, and routing policies are consistent across the primary and secondary sites, allowing for a smooth transition during a disaster recovery event.

Data consistency is another critical factor in disaster recovery planning for virtual machines. Many virtualized environments run complex applications such as databases or file servers, where data consistency is vital for business continuity. Virtual machines running such applications must be carefully managed during backup and replication to ensure that data is captured in a consistent state. Application-aware backups are necessary to ensure that database transactions or other critical processes are not left in an inconsistent state during the backup process. By integrating disaster recovery solutions with application-level APIs, administrators can ensure that VMs running critical applications are protected without the risk of data corruption during recovery.

Testing is an often-overlooked but vital part of disaster recovery planning. Even the best-designed recovery strategies can fail if they are not properly tested. Regular testing ensures that the disaster recovery plan works as expected and that all components, including backups, replication, failover, and network connectivity, are functioning correctly. Testing also provides an opportunity to identify potential weaknesses in the recovery plan and make adjustments before a real disaster occurs. Many organizations perform disaster recovery drills periodically to simulate various failure scenarios and ensure that the recovery process can be completed within the defined recovery time objectives (RTO) and recovery point objectives (RPO). These tests help ensure that the organization can recover quickly and efficiently in the event of an actual disaster.

Additionally, disaster recovery planning for virtual machines must consider the recovery of not only data but also the security of the virtualized environment. Virtual machines are susceptible to cyber threats, and any disaster recovery plan must include measures to protect against data breaches, ransomware, and other malicious attacks. Security measures such as encryption, access controls, and regular patching must be incorporated into the disaster recovery strategy to ensure that data is not compromised during recovery operations. Ensuring that backups and replicas are encrypted both at rest and in transit is critical for protecting sensitive information from unauthorized access.

Finally, as organizations move toward hybrid and multi-cloud environments, disaster recovery planning for virtual machines must extend across these environments. The ability to failover and recover VMs between on-premises data centers and public or private clouds adds an additional layer of complexity to disaster recovery strategies. Integrating cloud-based disaster recovery solutions with on-premises virtualized infrastructure enables organizations to take advantage of the scalability and flexibility of cloud platforms while maintaining control over their on-premises systems. By leveraging cloud resources for disaster recovery, organizations can achieve greater redundancy and ensure that they can recover quickly from a disaster, regardless of where their primary infrastructure resides.

Disaster recovery planning with virtual machines is an essential aspect of ensuring the continuity of business operations in the event of a failure or disaster. Through the use of replication, failover, backup, and orchestration, organizations can create robust and effective recovery strategies that minimize downtime and protect critical data. As virtualized environments become more complex and interconnected, disaster recovery planning must adapt to address new challenges, including cloud integration, network configuration, and data consistency. Properly implemented disaster recovery strategies ensure that virtualized infrastructures are resilient, secure, and capable of recovering quickly to maintain operational continuity.

Virtual Machine Performance Tuning

Virtual machine performance tuning is an essential part of optimizing virtualized environments to ensure that virtual machines (VMs) are running efficiently and meet the needs of the applications they host. With the increasing reliance on virtualized infrastructures, especially in cloud computing and data centers, ensuring the optimal performance of VMs becomes crucial for maintaining system stability, user satisfaction, and resource efficiency. Virtual machine performance tuning involves a combination of techniques to improve resource allocation, minimize bottlenecks, and maximize the use of available hardware resources. These adjustments are necessary not only to prevent performance degradation but also to provide the scalability and flexibility required by modern applications.

The first step in performance tuning for virtual machines is understanding the key resources that affect VM performance. These resources include CPU, memory, storage, and network bandwidth. Each of these components plays a critical role in how a VM performs, and resource allocation must be balanced to ensure that VMs do not experience contention or excessive resource usage. CPU performance is a key factor in VM responsiveness and the ability to handle workloads. The number of virtual CPUs (vCPUs) assigned to a VM must be carefully considered based on the workload it will handle. Overprovisioning vCPUs can lead to unnecessary overhead, as the hypervisor will need to manage more vCPUs than the host can efficiently handle. On the other hand, underprovisioning vCPUs can result in resource bottlenecks, especially for resource-intensive applications. Properly balancing the number of vCPUs assigned to each VM ensures that performance is optimized and resource contention is minimized.

Memory allocation is another critical aspect of performance tuning for virtual machines. VMs rely on virtual memory, which is mapped to the physical memory of the host machine. If a VM is allocated too much memory, it can cause unnecessary memory consumption, leading to inefficient use of host resources. Conversely, underallocating memory can cause the VM to use swap space or memory ballooning, which significantly degrades performance. In virtualized environments, memory overcommitment can lead to performance degradation if too many VMs are competing for limited physical memory resources. Administrators must monitor memory usage and adjust the allocated memory based on the needs of the VM's workload. Memory management features such as memory ballooning, transparent page sharing, and swapping should also be carefully configured to ensure that VMs perform optimally without consuming excessive host resources.

Storage performance is equally important when tuning virtual machines. Virtual disks in VMs are essentially files stored on the host system's storage devices, and the performance of these disks can significantly impact the performance of the VM. Slow disk I/O can cause applications running on the VM to lag, and it can also affect tasks like booting the operating system or accessing application data. Proper storage configuration is essential to prevent I/O bottlenecks. In virtualized environments, storage should be configured to ensure that each VM has access to fast, high-throughput storage, whether through local disks, network-attached storage (NAS), or storage area networks (SANs). Storage performance can also be enhanced through the use of solid-state drives (SSDs), which offer faster read/write speeds compared to traditional hard drives. Administrators should also consider storage policies such as thin provisioning or deduplication to optimize storage usage and prevent performance issues caused by insufficient disk space.

Networking performance also plays a significant role in virtual machine performance tuning. VMs rely on virtual network adapters to communicate with each other and with external resources, and network bottlenecks can severely degrade performance. Network latency and throughput issues can impact the performance of applications and services running on VMs, especially those that rely on real-time data transmission, such as web servers, databases, or streaming services. Administrators must ensure that VMs are connected to high-performance virtual switches and that network bandwidth is allocated appropriately across the virtualized environment. Additionally, configuring proper network isolation and segmentation can prevent network congestion and improve overall performance. Features such as Quality of Service (QoS) and network load balancing can help manage network traffic and ensure that critical applications receive the necessary bandwidth for optimal performance.

To optimize the performance of virtual machines, administrators should also monitor and adjust the virtual machine's resource allocation based on its usage patterns. Virtual machine monitoring tools allow administrators to track resource utilization in real-time, providing valuable insights into CPU, memory, storage, and network performance. These tools can identify resource bottlenecks, spikes in usage, or underutilization of resources. By analyzing these metrics, administrators can make informed decisions about resource allocation and adjust the number of vCPUs, memory allocation, or disk I/O throughput to better align with the VM's workload requirements. Additionally, monitoring tools can help detect performance degradation before it affects end users, allowing administrators to proactively address issues and prevent downtime.

Another important aspect of VM performance tuning is ensuring that the underlying hypervisor and host system are properly configured and optimized. The hypervisor manages the VMs and allocates resources from the physical host to each VM. If the hypervisor is not properly tuned or if the host system is underpowered or overloaded, it can negatively impact VM performance. Administrators must ensure that the host system has enough resources to support the number of VMs running on it. This includes optimizing CPU scheduling, memory management, and storage allocation. Host-level optimizations, such as enabling hardware virtualization features, adjusting processor affinity, and configuring resource pools, can help ensure that VMs perform efficiently and that host resources are used optimally.

Scaling and load balancing are also critical considerations in virtual machine performance tuning. As the number of VMs in an environment grows, administrators must ensure that the system remains scalable and that resource allocation is balanced across hosts. Load balancing involves distributing workloads evenly across the available resources to prevent overloading individual hosts while ensuring that VMs are allocated sufficient resources. Load balancing can be automated through resource management tools and hypervisor features, ensuring that VMs are dynamically moved or resized based on resource demands. This helps to maintain consistent performance, even as workloads change over time.

Additionally, resource contention between VMs is a common challenge in virtualized environments, especially when multiple VMs share the same physical hardware. Administrators must ensure that resources such as CPU and memory are allocated appropriately to avoid conflicts between VMs. Resource contention can be mitigated through techniques such as CPU pinning, where specific vCPUs are assigned to physical CPU cores, or by using resource limits and reservations to control the allocation of resources. These strategies help ensure that each VM receives the necessary resources while minimizing the impact on other VMs running on the same host.

Virtual machine performance tuning is an ongoing process that requires regular monitoring, adjustment, and optimization to ensure that virtualized environments remain efficient and responsive to changing business needs. Administrators must continuously assess resource utilization, monitor performance metrics, and adjust configurations to ensure that each VM operates at its best. By optimizing CPU, memory, storage, and network resources, administrators can improve the overall performance of virtual machines, enhance scalability, and ensure that virtualized environments remain reliable, responsive, and cost-effective. Effective performance tuning allows organizations to fully leverage the benefits of virtualization, ensuring that workloads are managed efficiently and that applications perform optimally in a virtualized environment.

Virtual Storage: Managing Disk and I/O

Virtual storage management is a critical component of a virtualized infrastructure, particularly as organizations continue to embrace virtualization for its efficiency, scalability, and flexibility. In virtual environments, managing disk and input/output (I/O) operations becomes increasingly complex because multiple virtual machines (VMs) share the same physical storage resources. As the number of VMs grows and workloads become more demanding, ensuring that virtual storage is managed effectively is vital for maintaining performance, reducing latency, and optimizing resource usage. The way storage is allocated and I/O operations are handled significantly impacts the overall performance and reliability of virtualized environments.

At the core of virtual storage management is the allocation of physical disk resources to virtual machines. In a typical virtualized setup, each VM has its own virtual disk, which is essentially a file that resides on the physical storage of the host system. The virtual disk behaves similarly to a physical disk from the VM's perspective, providing storage for the operating system, applications, and data. However, since virtual disks are files stored on the host's physical disk, managing the I/O between the VM's virtual disk and the underlying physical storage can introduce challenges related to performance, storage utilization, and resource contention.

One of the primary challenges in virtual storage management is ensuring that disk I/O operations are handled efficiently. Virtual machines generate disk I/O as they read and write data to their virtual disks. These I/O operations can involve a wide range of activities, from booting the VM, loading applications, to reading and writing large datasets. Since all VMs share the same physical storage resources, the I/O operations from multiple VMs can compete for access to the same physical disk, potentially leading to performance bottlenecks. This is particularly true in environments where resource-intensive applications are running on multiple VMs, as the increased demand for disk access can overwhelm the host's storage subsystem, leading to high latency, slow application performance, and reduced throughput.

To mitigate I/O bottlenecks and ensure optimal disk performance, administrators must carefully manage the allocation of storage resources. One approach to improving storage performance in virtualized environments is through the use of Storage Area Networks (SANs) or Network-Attached Storage (NAS). These centralized storage solutions provide high-performance shared storage to multiple VMs, allowing them to access data more efficiently than if they were relying on local storage attached to individual hosts. By centralizing storage and enabling fast data access, SAN and NAS solutions help ensure that disk I/O is distributed across a larger pool of storage resources, reducing the likelihood of bottlenecks and improving overall performance.

Another important aspect of virtual storage management is the use of storage provisioning techniques. Thin provisioning and thick provisioning are two common methods used to allocate storage to virtual machines. Thin provisioning allows for more efficient use of storage resources by allocating only the amount of storage that is actually being used by the virtual disk, rather than allocating the full disk size upfront. This can help prevent over-allocation of storage, especially in environments where multiple VMs are running on the same host. However, thin provisioning comes with the risk of running out of physical storage if the allocated storage exceeds the available capacity. Administrators must carefully monitor storage utilization to ensure that thin provisioning does not result in overcommitment.

Thick provisioning, on the other hand, allocates the full disk size to a VM upfront, reserving the storage even if it is not fully used. This can provide more predictable performance, as the storage is fully allocated and reserved, but it can lead to inefficiencies if the allocated storage is not fully utilized. Choosing between thin and thick provisioning depends on the specific use case and performance requirements of the virtualized environment. In general, thin provisioning is preferred for environments where storage efficiency is a priority, while thick provisioning is preferred for mission-critical applications that require consistent and predictable performance.

In addition to provisioning techniques, storage tiering is another method used to optimize storage performance. Storage tiering involves using different types of storage media, such as solid-state drives (SSDs) and traditional hard disk drives (HDDs), to store data based on its performance requirements. Frequently accessed data, or "hot" data, can be stored on high-performance SSDs, while less frequently accessed data, or "cold" data, can be stored on slower HDDs. This approach ensures that high-performance storage resources are allocated where they are most needed, while still allowing for cost-effective storage of less critical data. Storage tiering can be implemented at both the VM and storage array levels, providing flexibility in managing I/O workloads across a virtualized environment.

Another critical consideration in virtual storage management is the impact of virtualization on I/O performance. The virtualization layer itself introduces additional overhead for I/O operations, as the hypervisor must manage the mapping of virtual disks to physical storage. This overhead can cause I/O operations to be slower compared to direct access to physical storage. To address this, hypervisors provide various features to optimize disk I/O, such as paravirtualized disk drivers, which reduce the overhead associated with virtualizing storage. These optimized drivers provide more direct communication between the VM and the storage subsystem, improving I/O performance and reducing latency. Additionally, administrators should ensure that the hypervisor and storage subsystem are properly configured to minimize overhead and maximize throughput.

Disk performance in a virtualized environment can also be affected by the number of VMs running on a given host and the overall resource contention within the system. As more VMs are added to a host, the demand for storage resources increases, which can lead to competition for I/O access. Load balancing techniques and resource allocation management can help mitigate these issues. For example, by distributing VMs more evenly across physical hosts or implementing resource pools, administrators can prevent individual hosts from becoming overloaded and ensure that storage resources are allocated more effectively. Monitoring tools can also be used to track I/O performance and identify potential bottlenecks in the storage system, allowing administrators to take corrective actions before performance degrades.

Another key component of virtual storage management is data protection. In virtualized environments, data loss can have significant consequences, particularly for business-critical applications. Virtual machine snapshots and replication are commonly used to protect against data loss and facilitate disaster recovery. Snapshots capture the state of a VM at a specific point in time, allowing for quick rollback in the event of a failure or corruption. Replication, on the other hand, involves creating copies of VMs and storing them in a secondary location, ensuring that data can be recovered in case of a primary site failure. Both snapshotting and replication must be carefully managed to ensure that data is consistently protected and available for restoration when needed.

Finally, as virtualized environments grow in scale and complexity, storage performance tuning becomes increasingly important. Administrators must regularly evaluate and adjust the configuration of storage systems to ensure optimal performance. This may involve fine-tuning storage arrays, optimizing disk scheduling, adjusting cache settings, and monitoring I/O patterns to identify potential inefficiencies. By proactively managing storage and I/O performance, administrators can prevent bottlenecks, ensure high availability, and provide a seamless experience for end users and applications.

Managing disk and I/O in virtualized environments is a complex but essential task. Proper provisioning, performance tuning, and data protection strategies ensure that virtual machines operate efficiently, with minimal disruption. By understanding the intricacies of virtual storage management and optimizing resource allocation, administrators can create an environment that supports high performance, scalability, and reliability for both individual VMs and the broader infrastructure.

Virtual Networking: Configuring Virtual Switches

Virtual networking plays a crucial role in the operation of virtualized environments, providing the connectivity that enables communication between virtual machines (VMs), physical machines, and external networks. At the heart of virtual networking is the virtual switch, a software-based network device that enables network traffic to flow between VMs on the same host, between VMs on different hosts, and with external network resources. Proper configuration of virtual switches is vital for ensuring that virtualized environments perform optimally, remain secure, and provide reliable network connectivity. Virtual switches function much like physical switches, but they operate within the virtualized infrastructure, allowing for more flexible and dynamic network configurations that are critical for cloud environments and large data centers.

A virtual switch connects VMs to each other and to external physical networks, allowing them to communicate both internally and externally. In a typical physical network, each device connects to a physical switch, which forwards network packets based on MAC addresses. Similarly, virtual switches enable communication between VMs by forwarding packets between virtual network adapters associated with each VM. These virtual switches also handle the management of network traffic, such as forwarding, switching, and routing, similar to the role of physical switches in traditional network environments. The primary advantage of using virtual switches is that they allow for the abstraction of networking from the physical hardware, providing greater flexibility and scalability in managing virtualized environments.

One of the key elements of virtual switch configuration is defining the network interfaces through which VMs can communicate. Virtual switches are typically connected to physical network adapters on the host system. These physical adapters provide connectivity to external networks, such as local area networks (LANs) or the internet. By connecting virtual switches to physical network interfaces, VMs can send and receive traffic to and from external devices. This enables VMs to access shared resources, communicate with other VMs across different hosts, or even interact with external network services. Depending on the virtual switch configuration, VMs can either be isolated within their own virtual network or be allowed to communicate with the broader network infrastructure.

Virtual switches can also be configured to create isolated network segments within a virtualized environment. This can be achieved through the use of Virtual Local Area Networks (VLANs), which allow administrators to segment network traffic based on business requirements, security policies, or workload types. VLANs are particularly useful in multi-tenant environments or when there is a need to isolate traffic for security or performance reasons. For example, VMs running in a testing environment can be isolated from production VMs by assigning them to different VLANs, reducing the risk of security breaches or performance issues. Virtual switches can be configured to support VLAN tagging, which ensures that network traffic is correctly segmented and directed based on VLAN policies.

Another important aspect of virtual switch configuration is security. Just as physical switches implement network security features such as access control lists (ACLs) and port security, virtual switches can also enforce security policies to protect virtualized environments from unauthorized access or malicious activity. Virtual switches can be configured to limit the types of network traffic that are allowed between VMs, ensure that VMs only communicate with trusted devices, and isolate traffic between different virtual networks. Features like port mirroring and traffic filtering can also be configured on virtual switches to monitor network traffic and detect potential threats. Additionally, integrating virtual switches with firewall solutions and intrusion detection systems (IDS) can further enhance the security of the network, ensuring that virtual machines are protected from external and internal threats.

Network performance is another critical consideration in virtual switch configuration. Virtual switches are responsible for managing network traffic between VMs and external networks, and their configuration can have a significant impact on network throughput and latency. For example, if a virtual switch is configured with insufficient resources or poor network adapter settings, network traffic may experience delays or congestion. To optimize network performance, administrators can configure virtual switches to support features such as load balancing and Quality of Service (QoS). Load balancing helps distribute network traffic evenly across multiple network interfaces, preventing any single interface from becoming overwhelmed with traffic. QoS settings can be used to prioritize certain types of traffic, ensuring that critical applications or services receive the bandwidth they need to perform optimally.

In larger virtualized environments, where multiple hosts are involved, configuring virtual switches to enable communication between VMs on different hosts is essential. This can be achieved through the use of distributed virtual switches (DVS). A distributed virtual switch is a virtual switch that spans across multiple physical hosts, allowing VMs running on different hosts to communicate with each other as if they were connected to the same switch. This provides administrators with a more centralized and efficient way to manage networking in large virtual environments. Distributed virtual switches also enable features like network load balancing and network monitoring, which are critical for maintaining high availability and performance across the entire virtualized infrastructure.

Virtual switch configuration must also take into account the underlying hardware infrastructure. For example, network adapters on the physical host must be configured to support the virtual switch's requirements, including features like jumbo frames, network teaming, and link aggregation. Network adapters should be chosen based on their performance characteristics, as well as their ability to handle the traffic demands of the virtualized environment. In some cases, physical network interfaces may need to be dedicated to specific VMs or virtual switches to ensure that performance is not degraded by shared resources.

The integration of virtual switches with software-defined networking (SDN) platforms is an emerging trend in modern data centers and cloud environments. SDN provides a more programmable and flexible approach to network management, allowing administrators to dynamically configure and control virtual networks through centralized software controllers. By integrating virtual switches with SDN platforms, organizations can gain greater control over their network traffic, automate network provisioning and management, and implement more granular security policies. SDN enables administrators to easily manage complex network topologies, make real-time adjustments to network configurations, and integrate network services with other components of the virtualized infrastructure.

Virtual switches also play a role in ensuring the availability and reliability of the network in virtualized environments. High availability features such as network failover and link redundancy can be configured on virtual switches to prevent network outages. If a network interface or link fails, virtual switches can automatically failover to a backup link, ensuring that network connectivity is maintained. Redundant network paths can also be established to improve fault tolerance and prevent network disruptions, which is particularly important in environments where uptime and service availability are critical.

The proper configuration of virtual switches is a key factor in the overall performance, security, and reliability of virtualized environments. By ensuring that virtual switches are configured correctly, administrators can optimize network performance, implement robust security policies, and enable seamless communication between VMs and external systems. Virtual switches provide the flexibility and scalability needed for modern IT infrastructures, but their configuration must be carefully managed to meet the demands of a growing, dynamic virtualized environment.

With the right configuration, virtual switches can help organizations fully leverage the benefits of virtualization, ensuring that their network infrastructure is efficient, secure, and capable of supporting the needs of modern applications and services.

Virtual Machine Template Management

Virtual machine (VM) template management is a key component of virtualized infrastructure management, enabling the efficient and consistent deployment of virtual machines across an organization. VM templates are pre-configured images of a virtual machine that include the operating system, applications, configurations, and settings necessary to deploy a fully functional VM. These templates are used as a blueprint to quickly create new virtual machines without having to manually install and configure the operating system and applications each time a new VM is required. VM template management plays a vital role in improving efficiency, ensuring consistency, and simplifying the overall management of virtualized environments.

One of the primary benefits of using VM templates is the ability to standardize deployments across a virtualized infrastructure. Templates ensure that each VM deployed from them is configured in the same way, eliminating the potential for configuration errors or inconsistencies. This is particularly important in large-scale environments, where manually configuring each VM would be time-consuming, error-prone, and difficult to maintain. By using templates, administrators can ensure that all VMs have the same configurations, software, and security settings, which is essential for maintaining a secure and stable environment. This uniformity also simplifies the process of patch management, as administrators only need to update the template to apply updates to all VMs deployed from it.

Creating and managing virtual machine templates begins with the creation of a base virtual machine that contains the operating system and any software or configurations required for the specific use case. This base VM is then customized to meet the needs of the environment, such as by installing applications, configuring network settings, and applying security policies. Once the base VM is properly configured, it is converted into a template, which can be used to deploy multiple VMs quickly. The template essentially acts as a snapshot of the VM at a specific point in time, capturing its exact state, including its software, settings, and configurations.

Template management involves more than just creating and deploying VM templates; it also requires maintaining and updating templates over time. As operating systems, applications, and security patches evolve, templates must be updated to reflect the latest versions and configurations. Regularly updating templates ensures that newly deployed VMs benefit from the most up-to-date software and security features, reducing the risk of vulnerabilities or compatibility issues. Additionally, administrators must monitor the performance and compatibility of VMs deployed from templates to ensure that they meet the organization's operational requirements. If a particular template is no longer suitable or has become outdated, administrators may need to retire it and create a new version with updated configurations and software.

Another important aspect of virtual machine template management is the handling of template versions. Over time, templates may evolve to support new features, applications, or configurations. Managing these versions effectively is crucial for maintaining a consistent and secure virtualized environment. Version control allows administrators to track changes to templates, ensuring that older templates can be preserved if needed for legacy applications or compatibility purposes. It also helps to ensure that the most current and appropriate template is used for new deployments, preventing issues that might arise from using outdated templates. Version control can also help mitigate the risks associated with template modifications, as administrators can roll back to a previous version if a template update causes problems.

One of the challenges of VM template management is dealing with the scale of virtualized environments. In large environments with hundreds or thousands of VMs, managing templates can become complex. Administrators must ensure that templates are properly organized and cataloged to avoid confusion or mistakes when deploying new VMs. A well-organized template library, with clear naming conventions and categorization, can significantly simplify this process. Template management tools and platforms often include features like search, filtering, and categorization to help administrators find and use the appropriate templates quickly and easily. Automating template deployment and management can also streamline the process, reducing the administrative overhead and minimizing the risk of errors.

Additionally, template management should be integrated with the broader automation and orchestration processes within the virtualized infrastructure. For example, integration with a cloud management platform or a provisioning tool can allow templates to be automatically deployed as part of larger workflows or provisioning processes. This integration ensures that VM deployment is consistent with organizational policies, security standards, and resource allocation strategies. Automated deployment from templates can significantly reduce the time required to provision new VMs, allowing for faster scaling of virtualized environments in response to changing business needs.

Storage considerations also play a key role in VM template management. Templates can consume a significant amount of storage, especially in environments where multiple templates are used for different types of virtual machines. As templates are essentially full copies of virtual machines, they can quickly add up in terms of storage requirements. Administrators must ensure that there is enough storage available for the templates, especially if they are using large or complex templates with multiple configurations. Deduplication and compression technologies can help reduce the storage footprint of templates, making them more manageable and cost-effective. Additionally, storing templates on high-performance storage solutions, such as solid-state drives (SSDs), can improve the speed at which templates are deployed, which is important in environments where rapid VM provisioning is critical.

Template management is also closely tied to security. Templates contain the full configuration of a virtual machine, including sensitive information such as user credentials, network configurations, and security settings. As a result, securing templates is of utmost importance. Templates should be stored in secure locations, with access controls to prevent unauthorized modifications or access. Additionally, administrators should ensure that templates are regularly scanned for vulnerabilities, malware, and compliance with security standards. When updating templates, it is important to ensure that any sensitive data or configurations are properly handled to avoid exposing critical information. Encryption can be used to protect templates during storage and transit, ensuring that they remain secure even if accessed by unauthorized parties.

Finally, performance tuning is an important consideration when managing VM templates. A template that performs well in one environment may not necessarily perform optimally in another. As a result, templates should be tested and optimized for the specific workloads they will support. Performance tuning may involve adjusting virtual hardware settings, optimizing disk I/O, or configuring network settings to ensure that the template provides the best possible performance. By taking the time to optimize templates for specific use cases, organizations can ensure that their virtual machines run efficiently, even in complex or high-demand environments.

Virtual machine template management is essential for ensuring the efficiency, security, and consistency of virtualized environments. By creating standardized templates, automating deployments, and keeping templates updated, organizations can significantly reduce the time and effort required to provision new virtual machines. Effective template management also enhances security by ensuring that VMs are consistently configured and compliant with organizational standards. Through proper management, templates can provide a powerful tool for streamlining virtual machine provisioning, maintaining consistency, and optimizing the performance of virtualized infrastructures.

Managing Virtual Machines in Hyper-Converged Infrastructure

Managing virtual machines (VMs) in hyper-converged infrastructure (HCI) requires a nuanced approach, as HCI represents a convergence of compute, storage, and networking in a single software-driven platform. Unlike traditional infrastructure, where these components are managed separately, hyper-converged systems integrate these elements into a unified architecture, simplifying management and offering flexibility, scalability, and resilience. The integration of these components allows organizations to scale up or down quickly to meet changing business needs. However, managing VMs in an HCI environment presents unique challenges, including the need to optimize resource utilization, ensure high availability, and handle storage and networking in a way that maintains performance and efficiency. Effectively managing VMs in HCI environments requires a deep understanding of the underlying infrastructure and the tools available for automation, monitoring, and optimization.

One of the key advantages of hyper-converged infrastructure is its ability to consolidate resources, simplifying the deployment and management of virtual machines. Traditional data center architectures often require separate management for compute, storage, and networking. In contrast, HCI integrates all these components into a single platform, which can be managed through a centralized interface. This consolidation reduces complexity, as administrators no longer need to manage separate silos of infrastructure. In the context of VM management, HCI enables administrators to provision and manage virtual machines more efficiently, with the ability to allocate resources dynamically based on the needs of the workloads. Since HCI uses a software-defined approach, the underlying infrastructure can be abstracted from the virtual machines, providing a more flexible and agile environment that can adapt to changing demands.

Virtual machine deployment in hyper-converged infrastructure begins with the allocation of resources from the integrated compute and storage nodes. In HCI, compute and storage resources are tied together, allowing for the easy scaling of virtual machines as demand increases. Virtual machine provisioning is streamlined, as the system automatically allocates the required compute, storage, and networking resources. This flexibility is a significant advantage for businesses looking to scale quickly, as VMs can be deployed with minimal manual intervention. The storage resources in an HCI system are typically distributed across multiple nodes, ensuring that data redundancy and availability are maintained even as VMs are scaled or migrated across different hosts. As such, the storage layer in HCI plays a critical role in

VM management, as it ensures that VMs have consistent and reliable access to data, even during infrastructure changes.

One of the challenges in managing VMs in hyper-converged infrastructure is ensuring optimal resource allocation. Since HCI is designed to scale horizontally, it provides flexibility in terms of adding or removing nodes based on resource demand. However, administrators need to carefully monitor resource utilization to avoid overprovisioning or underprovisioning of resources. Overprovisioning can lead to wasted resources, while underprovisioning can result in performance bottlenecks. Hyper-converged systems typically come with built-in monitoring and management tools that provide real-time insights into resource usage, allowing administrators to track CPU, memory, storage, and networking utilization across the entire system. By continuously monitoring these metrics, administrators can ensure that virtual machines are allocated the appropriate resources and that the HCI platform is operating efficiently.

In addition to resource allocation, ensuring high availability is another critical aspect of managing virtual machines in an HCI environment. Hyper-converged infrastructure is designed to offer built-in redundancy, so VMs are protected from hardware failures. Data replication and distributed storage across multiple nodes in the HCI cluster ensure that data is always available, even if a host or node fails. In the event of a failure, virtual machines can be automatically moved or restarted on healthy hosts, minimizing downtime and maintaining business continuity. This level of availability is essential for organizations that rely on VMs for mission-critical workloads, as it ensures that services remain operational even in the face of hardware or software failures. High availability in HCI environments is typically achieved through features like automated VM failover and live migration, which are facilitated by the underlying infrastructure's ability to abstract hardware and provide seamless resource allocation across the cluster.

Another aspect of managing VMs in hyper-converged infrastructure is network management. In HCI, networking is integrated with compute and storage resources, providing a streamlined approach to network provisioning and management. Network bandwidth and connectivity are critical to ensuring that virtual machines can communicate with each other and with external systems. In a hyper-converged environment, virtual switches and network adapters are used to manage the flow of data between VMs, hosts, and external networks. Proper configuration of these network components is essential to avoid performance degradation or bottlenecks. Software-defined networking (SDN) is often used in HCI environments to provide more control over network traffic, allowing administrators to configure network policies and optimize traffic flow based on workload requirements.

To maintain optimal performance, HCI environments often implement automated load balancing. Load balancing ensures that VMs are evenly distributed across the available hosts, preventing any single host from becoming overwhelmed with too many resource demands. In addition to distributing VMs evenly, load balancing also helps with resource optimization by ensuring that workloads are running on hosts with the most available resources. This helps avoid situations where some VMs are starved for resources while others are overprovisioned. Load balancing, combined with dynamic resource allocation, ensures that virtual machines have the resources they need to perform efficiently, even as workloads change or new VMs are deployed.

Data protection is a critical consideration in managing virtual machines within a hyper-converged infrastructure. Since VMs contain critical business data, it is essential to implement robust backup and disaster recovery solutions to protect against data loss. Hyper-converged systems typically integrate data protection features such as automated backups, snapshots, and replication. Snapshots provide point-in-time copies of VMs, allowing administrators to quickly restore VMs to a previous state in case of data corruption or system failure. Additionally, replication features allow VMs to be backed up to remote locations or cloud storage, ensuring that data is protected from local disasters. These data protection mechanisms are critical for maintaining business continuity and ensuring that VMs can be quickly restored if needed.

Managing virtual machines in a hyper-converged infrastructure also involves ongoing maintenance and optimization. As the virtualized environment grows and evolves, administrators must continually assess the performance and resource utilization of the VMs. This may involve adjusting resource allocations, migrating VMs between hosts, and updating templates or configurations to reflect changes in workload requirements. Regular monitoring and performance tuning are essential to ensure that virtual machines are performing at their best and that the infrastructure remains scalable and resilient. Automation tools and orchestration platforms can be used to streamline these tasks, reducing the administrative burden and ensuring that VMs are managed consistently and efficiently.

Managing virtual machines in hyper-converged infrastructure requires careful planning, monitoring, and optimization. By leveraging the integrated resources of HCI, administrators can deploy, scale, and manage virtual machines with greater efficiency and flexibility than in traditional infrastructure. The benefits of hyper-converged systems, including improved resource utilization, high availability, and simplified management, make them an attractive choice for organizations looking to optimize their virtualized environments. However, ensuring that the underlying infrastructure is configured properly and that resources are allocated efficiently is key to maintaining optimal performance and minimizing downtime. With the right tools and practices, managing virtual machines in HCI environments can be a highly effective and scalable solution for modern IT infrastructures.

Managing Containers and Virtual Machines Together

The rise of containers alongside virtual machines (VMs) has revolutionized the way organizations deploy and manage applications. Containers, which encapsulate applications and their dependencies into lightweight, portable units, offer flexibility, scalability, and rapid deployment. Virtual machines, on the other hand, provide more isolation and resource allocation flexibility by running entire operating systems on top of the host system. While both containers and virtual machines are used for application deployment, they serve different purposes and come with their own advantages. However, as businesses strive to optimize their infrastructure, managing containers and virtual machines together has become essential for providing an integrated solution that capitalizes on the strengths of both technologies. This approach ensures a more efficient use of resources, streamlined management, and an environment that can support diverse workloads and application requirements.

The core difference between containers and virtual machines lies in how they use system resources. Virtual machines are isolated from each other and from the host system, running separate operating systems for each instance, which leads to higher resource consumption but greater flexibility and security. Containers, however, share the host operating system's kernel, which makes them much more lightweight and efficient in terms of resource utilization, but they do not provide the same level of isolation as VMs. Containers are often seen as a better fit for microservices architectures, where small, independent units of an application are deployed and scaled rapidly. VMs, on the other hand, are ideal for monolithic applications that require complete operating system environments, including specific configurations or legacy systems.

As organizations move towards hybrid environments that incorporate both containers and virtual machines, the challenge becomes how to manage both effectively. The goal is to combine the efficiency and scalability of containers with the security, isolation, and flexibility provided by virtual machines. This requires sophisticated orchestration tools, platforms, and management strategies to ensure that both VMs and containers work harmoniously within the same infrastructure. Platforms such as Kubernetes, OpenShift, and VMware vSphere are increasingly being used to bridge the gap between containers and virtual machines, allowing administrators to manage both in a unified manner.

One of the primary challenges in managing containers and virtual machines together is ensuring that the underlying infrastructure can support both technologies simultaneously. Containers are typically deployed on hosts with container runtimes such as Docker, while virtual machines are deployed on hypervisors like VMware, Hyper-V, or KVM. These systems require different methods of managing resources, networking, and storage. The complexity arises when administrators must configure shared resources, networking, and storage systems in a way that allows both containers and VMs to coexist efficiently. This includes ensuring that the storage systems are compatible with both VM disk images and container data volumes and that network configurations allow for seamless communication between containers, VMs, and external resources.

To effectively manage containers and virtual machines together, administrators need to implement a consistent approach to resource allocation. Virtual machines often require significant compute, memory, and storage resources due to the full operating systems they run. Containers, while lightweight, still require resources for application execution, and if not properly managed, they can overwhelm the host system's available resources. Therefore, administrators must balance the allocation of resources between VMs and containers to ensure that neither is starved of the necessary resources. This may involve using resource pools or managing resource quotas to prevent one type of workload from dominating the infrastructure.

Another important consideration is ensuring the network connectivity between containers and virtual machines. In traditional VM environments, network communication is isolated, and VMs communicate with each other through virtual switches or physical network interfaces. Containers, however, can sometimes introduce complexities in networking, especially when they are spread across multiple hosts in a container orchestration platform like Kubernetes. To bridge the gap, administrators need to configure virtual networks that can handle both VM traffic and container traffic, ensuring that both types of workloads can communicate without performance degradation. This often involves using software-defined networking (SDN) solutions that allow the network to be dynamically reconfigured to accommodate both container and VM traffic as it scales.

Security is another critical factor when managing containers and virtual machines together. While both containers and VMs offer isolation, containers do so at the application level, whereas VMs provide a stronger, more traditional form of isolation at the hardware level. Managing security across both containers and VMs requires ensuring that the right security policies are in place to protect against vulnerabilities in both types of workloads. Administrators must deploy security solutions that can protect both containerized applications and virtual machine environments, including firewalls, intrusion detection systems, and security scans for both container images and VM instances. Additionally, ensuring that containers do not share sensitive information or access to resources between VMs is vital to prevent cross-container or cross-VM attacks.

When it comes to automation and orchestration, both containers and virtual machines benefit from streamlined workflows that reduce manual intervention and enhance efficiency. Containers are often orchestrated using tools like Kubernetes, which automates the deployment, scaling, and management of containerized applications. Similarly, virtual machine management platforms like VMware vSphere provide automation capabilities for VM provisioning, lifecycle management, and scaling. To manage both containers and VMs together, many organizations are turning to hybrid orchestration platforms that integrate both container orchestration tools like Kubernetes and VM management tools like vSphere. These platforms enable unified management of both containerized and virtualized workloads, allowing administrators to automate the deployment and scaling of both types of resources while maintaining consistency and security.

Another aspect to consider when managing containers and virtual machines together is storage management. In traditional virtualized environments, storage is often managed through centralized storage systems such as SANs or NAS, which are shared across all VMs. For containerized applications, persistent storage is necessary for storing application data, and while containers are inherently ephemeral, they can still require access to persistent storage. Technologies like container storage interfaces (CSI) are used to allow containers to use external storage resources. Managing both types of storage—whether for VMs or containers—requires a unified approach that ensures storage is efficiently allocated, high-performing, and resilient to failures. Virtual storage systems must be configured to handle both the high I/O demands of virtual machines and the dynamic storage requirements of containers.

The integration of monitoring and logging tools across both containers and virtual machines is also essential for managing hybrid environments. With containers, monitoring typically involves tracking metrics related to containers themselves, such as container uptime, resource consumption, and network traffic. For virtual machines, the focus is often on metrics related to VM health, resource utilization, and network performance. Tools like Prometheus, Grafana, and ELK Stack are commonly used in containerized environments to collect and visualize data. For virtual machines, traditional monitoring solutions like vCenter or other hypervisor-based tools are typically used. To manage both types of workloads efficiently, administrators need to integrate these monitoring systems, ensuring that both container and VM metrics are visible in a centralized platform that provides insights into the overall health of the infrastructure.

Managing containers and virtual machines together is a critical part of modern infrastructure management. By integrating the strengths of both technologies—containers for rapid deployment and scalability, and virtual machines for isolation and resource flexibility—organizations can create more efficient, resilient, and scalable environments. However, this requires careful planning and a deep understanding of the unique challenges each technology presents. Ensuring proper resource allocation, network connectivity, security, and orchestration between containers and VMs allows organizations to leverage both technologies effectively and maximize the potential of their virtualized and containerized environments.

The Role of Virtualization in DevOps

Virtualization plays a crucial role in DevOps, a methodology that promotes collaboration between development and operations teams to increase the speed and quality of software delivery. By abstracting the underlying hardware, virtualization provides a flexible, scalable, and cost-efficient environment that is essential for the dynamic, fast-paced needs of DevOps practices. In a DevOps pipeline, where software is continuously developed, tested, and deployed, virtualization supports automation, testing, scalability, and resource management. It allows DevOps teams to create isolated environments, run parallel development streams, and ensure consistency across various stages of the software lifecycle.

At the heart of DevOps is the need to accelerate the development and deployment of applications. Virtualization facilitates this by providing an isolated environment where applications can be developed, tested, and deployed independently from the underlying infrastructure. Virtual machines (VMs) or containers can be quickly created, customized, and destroyed, making it possible to replicate environments quickly and ensure that software is tested in conditions that closely mirror production. For example, developers can work in virtual environments that mimic the final deployment target, ensuring that the software behaves as expected when it reaches production. This isolation ensures that developers are not limited by physical machines or configurations, which allows for greater flexibility and efficiency in application development and testing.

One of the most significant ways that virtualization supports DevOps is by enabling continuous integration and continuous delivery (CI/CD). CI/CD are core practices in DevOps that focus on automating the integration of code changes and delivering applications to production in a streamlined manner. Virtualization helps implement CI/CD pipelines by providing automated environments where code can be tested in parallel across multiple VMs or containers. These virtual environments can be easily provisioned and decommissioned, allowing teams to run tests in a consistent, reproducible manner. Virtual machines or containers are ideal for running automated tests, as they can be configured to replicate various configurations or operating systems. For instance, a VM can be provisioned with the exact configuration needed to test a particular aspect of the application, whether that's a specific OS, environment, or version of a tool. Virtualization allows for this testing to occur in an automated, repeatable process without requiring extensive manual setup.

Virtualization also plays a key role in resource management within a DevOps workflow. By using virtualized environments, teams can allocate resources as needed, ensuring that they are not constrained by physical hardware limitations. Virtualization allows for more efficient resource allocation by enabling the dynamic scaling of environments. When additional compute power or storage is required, new VMs or containers can be spun up quickly, and when resources are no longer needed, they can be shut down just as easily. This flexibility allows DevOps teams to allocate resources based on workload demands, ensuring that testing, development, and deployment can continue without delay. Virtualization also makes it possible to isolate resources for different stages of the DevOps pipeline, preventing resource contention and ensuring that testing and production environments remain stable and performant.

Another important benefit of virtualization in DevOps is its ability to ensure consistency across different environments. Developers often encounter the problem of software working in their local environment but failing in production. This is frequently due to differences in configuration between the two environments. Virtualization addresses this problem by allowing teams to create identical environments that can be replicated throughout the development, testing, and production stages. By using the same virtual machines or containers for each stage of the process, teams can ensure that code behaves consistently across different environments. Virtual machines are especially useful here because they can be cloned or deployed in exact replicas, creating a controlled environment that mirrors production closely. Containers also offer a similar benefit by ensuring that applications and their dependencies are packaged together, eliminating any discrepancies between development and production configurations.

Virtualization supports collaboration between development and operations teams, which is a cornerstone of the DevOps methodology. In traditional IT operations, environments are typically managed in silos, with developers working on their machines and operations teams handling deployment on physical servers. This separation often leads to bottlenecks, communication breakdowns, and inefficiencies. Virtualization, however, creates a unified environment where both developers and operations teams can work together seamlessly. For example, developers can use containers or VMs to develop and test applications in an environment that can be easily replicated by operations teams for deployment. Likewise, operations teams can manage and configure virtualized environments centrally, ensuring that resources are provisioned quickly and efficiently. The shared virtual environments foster collaboration and communication between teams, helping to break down traditional silos and accelerate the delivery of software.

Moreover, virtualization provides a cost-effective solution for DevOps practices. Running multiple instances of virtual machines or containers on a single physical host allows organizations to maximize their hardware utilization, reducing the need for additional physical infrastructure. This is especially beneficial for DevOps teams, as they often require numerous test and development environments that can be costly to provision on physical hardware. By using virtualized environments, organizations can reduce capital expenditures on hardware and improve the efficiency of their infrastructure. The ability to scale up or down quickly without requiring additional physical servers also reduces operational costs and enhances agility. This cost-effectiveness is particularly valuable in dynamic, fast-moving environments where software needs to be delivered quickly and frequently.

Security is also an important consideration when using virtualization in DevOps. While virtual environments provide a level of isolation between applications and underlying infrastructure, it is essential for teams to ensure that security is integrated into the DevOps pipeline. Virtualization enables the creation of secure, isolated environments for testing and deployment, ensuring that vulnerabilities in one part of the application do not compromise the rest of the infrastructure. Additionally, security policies can be applied at the virtual machine or container level, ensuring that each environment meets security standards before it is deployed into production. With the ability to isolate applications, control access, and enforce security policies within virtual environments, virtualization can help DevOps teams address security concerns and minimize the risk of breaches.

The integration of virtualization into the DevOps process has far-reaching effects on the speed, efficiency, and scalability of software delivery. By providing the tools for creating isolated environments, enabling automation of CI/CD pipelines, optimizing resource management, and ensuring consistency across environments, virtualization accelerates the development lifecycle and enables organizations to deploy high-quality software faster. It also fosters collaboration between development and operations teams, helping to streamline workflows and improve communication. As organizations continue to embrace DevOps practices, virtualization will remain an essential technology for enabling the flexibility, scalability, and consistency required to meet the demands of modern software development and deployment.

Virtualization for Testing and Development Environments

Virtualization has fundamentally transformed the way development and testing environments are set up and managed. With traditional infrastructure, creating isolated, dedicated environments for every test or development scenario could be a costly and time-consuming endeavor. However, with virtualization, development and testing teams can create flexible, scalable environments that mimic production systems without the need for physical hardware. This capability significantly accelerates the software development lifecycle, allowing for rapid testing, bug fixes, and iteration while maintaining a high level of consistency and reliability.

The primary benefit of using virtualization for testing and development environments is its ability to quickly provision isolated environments. Virtualization abstracts the underlying physical hardware, enabling multiple virtual machines (VMs) or containers to run on a single host. This allows teams to create multiple environments with different configurations on a single physical server, reducing hardware costs and space requirements. Developers and testers can provision these environments with a few simple commands, instantly setting up different operating systems, application versions, or configurations without the need for new physical machines. This flexibility is especially valuable in environments where testing requires different setups or configurations for various versions of the application being developed.

In testing environments, virtualization also offers the ability to create snapshots of virtual machines. Snapshots are point-in-time copies of the virtual machine's state, capturing everything from the operating system to the application and data within it. These snapshots can be taken before or after specific tests are run, allowing testers to quickly revert to a known, stable state if an issue arises. For example, if a test leads to a configuration issue or a software bug that disrupts the environment, a snapshot can be restored with minimal effort, ensuring that testing can continue without delays. This reduces the overhead of manually reconfiguring or reinstalling environments, making the testing process more efficient and less prone to errors.

Another critical advantage of virtualization in testing and development is its ability to easily replicate production environments. Testing environments that closely mirror production are vital for catching bugs or performance issues that might not be apparent in local or development setups. By using virtualization, teams can deploy virtual machines that replicate the production environment, ensuring that tests are carried out in conditions that are as close to real-world use as possible. These virtualized replicas can simulate the same configurations, network settings, and even the same scale of resources as production, providing developers and testers with a true-to-life environment for their work. This capability helps in identifying issues that might otherwise go unnoticed in more isolated or unrealistic test environments, such as performance degradation, load balancing problems, or compatibility issues between different systems.

Virtualization also enhances the scalability of development and testing environments. In traditional setups, scaling requires adding physical hardware, which can be both costly and time-consuming. With virtualization, environments can be scaled up or down with ease. If a development team needs additional environments for simultaneous workstreams or if testing requires simulating a high load of virtual machines, this can be done by provisioning more VMs quickly. Similarly, if fewer resources are needed, virtual machines can be decommissioned without the need for hardware disposal or reconfiguration. This scalability ensures that development and testing environments can adapt to the dynamic needs of the project without significant delays or additional costs.

Moreover, virtualization allows for more efficient resource utilization. In traditional environments, each physical machine is typically dedicated to one function, whether it's running a particular development task or hosting a testing environment. In a virtualized environment, however, multiple VMs or containers can share the same physical resources, optimizing server capacity. This leads to better use of compute, memory, and storage resources, as multiple development and testing tasks can run concurrently on the same hardware. This optimization reduces the overall infrastructure footprint and helps organizations save on hardware and operational costs. Furthermore, because virtualized environments are often more lightweight than traditional setups, they can be spun up and down faster, making them ideal for quick, iterative testing and development.

In the context of DevOps and Agile development methodologies, virtualization provides critical support for continuous integration and continuous delivery (CI/CD) pipelines. These methodologies emphasize frequent integration of code changes and rapid deployment, both of which depend on reliable and efficient testing environments. Virtual machines and containers can be integrated into automated CI/CD pipelines to ensure that code is tested and validated quickly before it moves to production. By leveraging virtualized environments, teams can run automated tests in parallel, reducing the time required for testing while ensuring that new code changes don't introduce defects into the system. This integration allows for faster feedback loops, making it easier to identify and fix issues early in the development cycle.

Security testing is another area where virtualization shines. Developers and testers often need to evaluate how applications behave under different security scenarios, such as in the presence of vulnerabilities or when subjected to attack simulations. Virtualization provides an isolated environment where such security tests can be conducted without risking damage to other parts of the infrastructure. Virtual machines can be configured with specific security tools, and environments can be isolated from production to prevent potential threats from spreading. Additionally, containers can be used to create sandboxed environments for testing malware or other potentially harmful software, ensuring that the system's integrity remains intact while conducting potentially dangerous tests.

Virtualization also provides a convenient way to manage multiple environments for different development or testing purposes. In large development teams, each team or individual may require a different setup depending on the software being developed, the operating system being used, or the specific version of the application being tested. Virtualization makes it easy to create tailored environments for each developer or testing scenario. Furthermore, these environments can be stored as templates, allowing for rapid provisioning of new environments with the desired configurations. This flexibility ensures that developers and testers have the exact setup they need, reducing the time spent on configuration and increasing the overall speed of the development and testing process.

Furthermore, virtualization is not limited to creating isolated environments for testing but can also extend to collaboration between development and testing teams. By using shared virtual environments, developers and testers can easily replicate each other's setups and work together more effectively. Testing environments can be synchronized with the development process, enabling teams to quickly test new features or bug fixes as they are being developed. This streamlined workflow fosters better communication and cooperation between the teams, aligning them with the overall goals of the software development process.

In testing and development environments, virtualization plays an essential role in improving efficiency, scalability, and cost-effectiveness. It allows for rapid provisioning and reconfiguration of environments, enhances the replication of production systems for more realistic testing, and ensures that resources are used efficiently. Virtualization's flexibility enables development and testing teams to work more effectively, ensuring higher-quality software and faster release cycles. It also supports the modern development practices of Agile and DevOps, providing a scalable and automated infrastructure that can adapt to the evolving demands of software development. By leveraging the benefits of virtualization, organizations can streamline their development and testing processes, ultimately leading to better products and more satisfied users.

Virtual Machine Licensing and Compliance

Virtual machine licensing and compliance are critical considerations for organizations utilizing virtualization technologies to deploy, manage, and scale their infrastructure. The virtualized environment offers tremendous flexibility, scalability, and cost efficiency. However, it also introduces complexities in terms of software licensing and ensuring compliance with the terms and conditions set by software vendors. As organizations increasingly rely on virtual machines (VMs) for production workloads, development, and testing, the need to understand and manage licensing models becomes more important than ever. Failure to properly manage VM licensing and ensure compliance can result in legal and financial repercussions, including penalties, audits, and disruptions to business operations.

Licensing for virtual machines is not always straightforward, as it depends on the type of software being used, the vendor's licensing model, and how the VMs are deployed. Traditional software licensing models, where licenses are tied to physical hardware or specific servers, do not always map well to virtualized environments. This is because VMs can be moved, cloned, or replicated easily, leading to challenges in tracking and ensuring that all instances are properly licensed. For instance, licensing models based on the number of CPUs or cores in a physical server can become complicated when VMs are moved between hosts with different configurations. Other licensing models, such as those based on the number of users or devices, may not easily account for the dynamic nature of virtual machines, especially in environments with frequent scaling.

Software vendors have responded to the challenges of virtualization by introducing licensing models that are specifically designed for virtualized environments. One common approach is to base licenses on the number of VMs, providing organizations with more predictable costs as they scale their infrastructure. In these cases, the licensing cost is determined by the number of virtual machines running specific software, regardless of the underlying physical hardware. Another model involves licensing based on the number of virtual processors (vCPUs) assigned to each virtual machine. This approach is more granular and allows for more flexibility in terms of resource allocation. Licensing by vCPU is typically used by vendors like Microsoft and Oracle, where the cost scales with the processing power allocated to the virtual machine.

Another licensing model that is commonly used in virtualized environments is the use of subscription-based licenses. Instead of purchasing perpetual licenses for each virtual machine or processor, organizations can pay on a subscription basis, typically annually or monthly. This model allows for greater flexibility in managing software costs, as it can be adjusted based on the number of active virtual machines or the number of resources being consumed at any given time. Subscription-based models are often used by cloud providers like Amazon Web Services (AWS) and Microsoft Azure, where users pay for the software they use on-demand. This approach aligns well with the elasticity of virtual environments, allowing organizations to scale their usage and costs according to their actual needs.

When it comes to licensing compliance, virtualization presents several unique challenges. One of the main issues is the ability to track and monitor software usage in a dynamic environment. Since VMs can be easily moved between hosts, duplicated, or spun up on demand, ensuring that each virtual machine is properly licensed can be difficult without a robust system in place for tracking and auditing usage. Virtual machine management platforms, such as VMware vSphere or Microsoft Hyper-V, often include tools for managing licenses and tracking VM instances. However, these tools may not always be sufficient, particularly in larger or more complex environments. Third-party software management tools that specialize in license tracking and compliance can be an invaluable resource, providing organizations with the ability to monitor and enforce compliance across their entire virtualized infrastructure.

One of the most important aspects of managing virtual machine licensing and compliance is understanding the software vendor's specific terms and conditions. Many vendors have specific rules regarding the deployment of their software in virtual environments, and failing to adhere to these rules can result in compliance violations. For example, some vendors require that licenses be tied to a specific host or physical server, even though the software is running on a virtual machine. In these cases, organizations may need to use special tools or licensing agreements that ensure the software is only used on the designated host. Other vendors may have more flexible licensing models that allow software to be freely deployed in virtual environments, but these models still require careful tracking to ensure compliance with the license terms.

One significant challenge in virtual machine licensing and compliance is the potential for software audits. Software vendors, especially those with traditional licensing models, may periodically audit organizations to ensure that they are using the software in compliance with the terms of the license agreement. These audits can be time-consuming and costly, especially if discrepancies are found between the number of licenses purchased and the number of instances in use. In a virtualized environment, where software can easily be replicated and moved between hosts, the risk of non-compliance increases, and organizations may be at risk of facing penalties or having to purchase additional licenses to cover unlicensed instances.

Organizations can mitigate the risks associated with software audits and compliance violations by establishing clear policies and procedures for license management. This includes keeping detailed records of all software licenses, the number of virtual machines running specific software, and the hardware resources allocated to each VM. Regularly auditing software usage within the virtualized environment and conducting internal compliance checks can help ensure that the organization stays on top of its licensing obligations. Additionally, using automated tools that track license usage and generate reports can help provide visibility into the organization's software usage and prevent unexpected compliance issues.

Virtualization platforms themselves may also have specific licensing requirements that need to be considered. For example, hypervisor software like VMware ESXi or Microsoft Hyper-V often requires separate licenses based on the number of physical hosts, cores, or processors. These licenses may be separate from the licenses required for the virtual machines running on top of the hypervisor. In these cases, organizations need to ensure that both the underlying virtualization platform and the software running on the virtual machines are properly licensed to avoid any compliance issues.

As cloud computing becomes more prevalent, virtual machine licensing and compliance are also becoming more complex. Public cloud providers, such as AWS, Azure, and Google Cloud, offer virtualized environments where organizations can provision and scale virtual machines on-demand. While this offers flexibility and scalability, it also introduces new licensing challenges. Many software vendors offer different licensing models for cloud environments, and these models may differ from those used in on-premises virtualized environments. Organizations need to understand how their licenses apply to cloud-based virtual machines and ensure that they comply with both the vendor's terms and the cloud provider's terms of service. Cloud providers often have tools to help manage licenses, but it remains the organization's responsibility to ensure that they are using the software in accordance with the licensing agreements.

The complexity of virtual machine licensing and compliance in virtualized and cloud environments requires careful planning and management. Organizations must understand the licensing models available, track software usage across dynamic virtualized environments, and implement processes to ensure that they remain compliant with vendor terms. Effective license management tools, coupled with regular audits and a thorough understanding of the vendor's policies, can help mitigate the risks of non-compliance and ensure that organizations can fully leverage the benefits of virtualization while avoiding costly penalties or legal disputes.

Virtualization with Open Source Hypervisors

Open source hypervisors have become an increasingly popular choice for organizations seeking cost-effective and flexible virtualization solutions. Unlike proprietary hypervisors, which often come with expensive licensing fees, open source hypervisors provide an alternative that can be customized, adapted, and used without the burden of ongoing costs. These hypervisors are typically built around the same core functionality as commercial products, offering robust features for creating and managing virtual machines (VMs), as well as supporting various operating systems and workloads. Virtualization with open source hypervisors offers significant advantages, particularly for organizations that require the flexibility to adapt to rapidly changing business needs or those with limited IT budgets.

The main advantage of using open source hypervisors is the cost-saving aspect. Licensing fees associated with proprietary hypervisors, like VMware vSphere or Microsoft Hyper-V, can add up quickly, especially when deploying at scale. Open source hypervisors, on the other hand, are available without these fees. This makes them particularly appealing to small and medium-sized enterprises (SMEs) or startups that may not have the resources to invest heavily in commercial virtualization technologies. By using open source hypervisors, organizations can free up resources for other areas of their IT infrastructure or development, reducing overall operational costs.

Another key benefit of open source hypervisors is the level of customization they offer. Many commercial hypervisors, while feature-rich, are relatively rigid in terms of configuration and management. Open source solutions, such as KVM (Kernel-based Virtual Machine), Xen, and VirtualBox, are designed with flexibility in mind. Users can modify the source code to meet their specific requirements, enabling tailored solutions that might not be possible with proprietary systems. This customization extends not only to the hypervisor itself but also to the management tools and interfaces that control the virtual environment. Organizations can integrate open source hypervisors into their existing infrastructure, adapt them to their specific workflows, and extend them with additional features as needed. This flexibility allows for greater innovation and optimization, especially in environments with unique or complex requirements.

Despite the many advantages, managing virtualized environments with open source hypervisors also requires careful planning and expertise. While these hypervisors are powerful, they often lack the comprehensive support and polished user interfaces that are available with commercial solutions. Users of open source hypervisors must be comfortable working with command-line tools, configuration files, and troubleshooting in environments where formal support might be limited. That said, the community-driven nature of many open source projects provides access to a vast repository of resources, documentation, and forums where users can seek help and share best practices. The support from the open-source community, while not as structured as commercial offerings, can be invaluable for administrators who are looking to maximize the potential of their virtualization infrastructure.

The open-source nature of these hypervisors also enables organizations to avoid vendor lock-in, which is a common concern with proprietary solutions. With commercial hypervisors, organizations often become dependent on a single vendor for updates, patches, and support. If the vendor changes its pricing model or product offerings, customers may be forced to adopt new terms or technologies, potentially disrupting their infrastructure. Open source hypervisors, on the other hand, allow organizations to maintain full control over their environment, avoiding the risks associated with vendor lock-in. This control also extends to security updates and patches, which can be applied independently, allowing for a more responsive approach to potential vulnerabilities. Open-source hypervisors are developed and maintained by a global community of contributors, which helps ensure that they stay up-to-date with the latest advancements and security features.

Security is an essential consideration in any virtualized environment, and open source hypervisors are no exception. Many open-source hypervisors have robust security features, including support for secure boot, virtualization-based isolation, and encryption. Additionally, the transparent nature of open-source software means that vulnerabilities can be identified and addressed more quickly than with closed-source systems, where security flaws might go unnoticed until they are exploited. For organizations that require a high level of security, open source hypervisors provide the ability to closely scrutinize the code and ensure that the virtualization environment is free from vulnerabilities. However, this level of control also means that administrators must take on a more proactive role in security management, regularly reviewing patches and ensuring that the hypervisor is configured securely.

In terms of functionality, open source hypervisors such as KVM and Xen are highly capable and support a wide range of guest operating systems, including Linux, Windows, and various Unix-based systems. These hypervisors provide many of the same features that are found in proprietary hypervisors, including virtual machine migration, resource management, and snapshot functionality. KVM, for example, is integrated into the Linux kernel, providing a lightweight and highly efficient virtualization solution for Linux-based environments. Xen, another open-source hypervisor, is known for its strong isolation features and is often used in cloud computing environments.

VirtualBox, though less scalable than KVM or Xen, provides a user-friendly interface for smaller-scale deployments and is commonly used for testing, development, or personal virtualization projects.

Open source hypervisors are also often used in conjunction with other open source technologies to create a fully integrated, cost-effective virtualization ecosystem. For instance, many organizations combine KVM with OpenStack, a popular open-source cloud computing platform, to build private clouds and manage large-scale virtualization environments. By leveraging the power of both open source hypervisors and orchestration tools like OpenStack, organizations can create flexible, dynamic infrastructures that can scale as needed, without the need for costly proprietary solutions. These open-source tools work together to offer a seamless experience for managing VMs, storage, networking, and other infrastructure components, providing a comprehensive solution for businesses that want to maintain control over their virtualized environments.

For businesses that need to scale their virtualized environments or deploy large numbers of virtual machines, open source hypervisors offer the necessary scalability. KVM and Xen are both capable of handling large-scale environments with hundreds or thousands of virtual machines. These hypervisors allow administrators to efficiently manage resources, allocate CPU and memory, and monitor performance across multiple hosts. With the help of automation tools and orchestration platforms, scaling virtual machine infrastructure becomes much more manageable, allowing organizations to add new hosts or VMs on demand and ensure that workloads are distributed evenly.

While open source hypervisors offer many benefits, they may not be suitable for every organization. Large enterprises or those with highly complex requirements may find that the lack of official support or the steep learning curve associated with some open-source solutions limits their effectiveness. Additionally, the absence of out-of-the-box tools for monitoring and managing the virtualized environment can make it more difficult to oversee large-scale deployments. In these cases, organizations may prefer proprietary hypervisors, which offer integrated management tools, enterprise-level support, and more polished user interfaces.

Virtualization with open source hypervisors has become a viable and appealing option for organizations seeking flexibility, cost-effectiveness, and control over their virtual environments. By leveraging open-source solutions like KVM, Xen, and VirtualBox, businesses can create customized virtualized infrastructures that meet their specific needs, avoid vendor lock-in, and scale as required. While open source hypervisors require a certain level of expertise and proactive management, they offer significant advantages for businesses that prioritize control, cost savings, and customization. With the continued growth of the open-source community, these hypervisors will continue to evolve, providing even more robust and reliable solutions for virtualization in various environments.

Scaling Virtual Machines in Cloud Environments

Scaling virtual machines (VMs) in cloud environments is a fundamental practice that allows businesses to manage dynamic workloads, optimize resource utilization, and ensure that applications perform efficiently under varying demand. The cloud provides a flexible and scalable infrastructure that makes it easier to adjust resources in real-time, allowing organizations to provision, resize, and terminate virtual machines based on current operational requirements. Cloud environments, with their distributed nature and on-demand resource availability, offer businesses the opportunity to scale their virtual infrastructure seamlessly. However, the ability to scale virtual machines effectively requires careful planning, understanding of cloud platforms, and the implementation of automation tools to maintain performance and control costs.

Cloud environments are inherently designed to handle scalability, whether horizontally or vertically. Horizontal scaling, also known as scaling out, involves adding more virtual machines to distribute the workload. Vertical scaling, or scaling up, refers to increasing the resources (such as CPU, memory, or storage) of an existing VM. Horizontal scaling is typically used when there is a need to handle more traffic or data without significantly altering the architecture of an application, while vertical scaling is used to improve the performance of an individual instance. Both approaches have their benefits and challenges, and selecting the right strategy depends on the nature of the workload, the application architecture, and the goals of the business.

In cloud environments, scaling virtual machines horizontally is often associated with distributed computing and containerized applications. When a service or application experiences increased demand, additional virtual machines can be spun up to handle the load, distributing the traffic across multiple instances. This is particularly useful in applications that are designed to be stateless, where the application logic and data are not tied to a specific instance. By adding more VMs, the application can distribute its processing load and increase throughput, reducing the likelihood of performance degradation due to resource exhaustion. One of the primary benefits of horizontal scaling in the cloud is its elasticity, as virtual machines can be added or removed automatically based on the traffic or processing requirements, allowing businesses to adapt quickly to changes in demand.

On the other hand, vertical scaling is often more suitable for applications that require greater computing power or memory but cannot be distributed across multiple VMs. By increasing the CPU, memory, or disk size of an existing VM, vertical scaling enhances the capacity of a single instance to handle more demanding workloads. Vertical scaling is commonly used in scenarios where a single VM needs more resources, such as databases or monolithic applications that are not designed to be horizontally scalable. However, vertical scaling has its limitations, as it is constrained by the maximum resource capacity available on a single machine, making it less flexible than horizontal scaling when dealing with very large or highly variable workloads.

Both horizontal and vertical scaling are supported by major cloud platforms like Amazon Web Services (AWS), Microsoft Azure, and Google Cloud Platform (GCP), each offering tools and services to automate the process. For instance, AWS provides services like Auto Scaling and Elastic Load Balancing to manage and scale EC2 instances, allowing virtual machines to automatically scale based on demand.

Azure offers Virtual Machine Scale Sets, which allow users to deploy and manage a group of load-balanced VMs that can automatically scale up or down based on traffic patterns. These automated scaling tools allow organizations to respond to changing workloads without requiring manual intervention, ensuring that resources are allocated efficiently, and operational costs are minimized.

While scaling virtual machines in the cloud offers many benefits, it also introduces several challenges. One of the primary challenges is ensuring that VMs are scaled appropriately based on the actual demand. In some cases, organizations may overestimate the resources required, leading to overprovisioning and unnecessary costs. Conversely, underestimating the demand can result in performance issues, such as slow response times or application crashes. Effective monitoring and performance analysis are essential to ensure that VMs are scaled in a way that matches the workload requirements. Cloud platforms provide robust monitoring tools, such as AWS CloudWatch, Azure Monitor, and GCP's Stackdriver, which can track resource utilization and performance metrics. These tools allow administrators to set thresholds and alerts, enabling them to automatically scale VMs up or down based on specific performance indicators, such as CPU usage, memory consumption, or network traffic.

Another challenge in scaling VMs in cloud environments is managing costs. While cloud infrastructure offers flexibility, the pay-as-you-go pricing model can lead to higher-than-expected costs if VMs are not properly managed. Vertical scaling, in particular, can become expensive if the cost of additional resources outpaces the benefits gained from improved performance. Horizontal scaling, while more cost-effective in some cases, requires managing multiple VMs, which can increase the complexity of infrastructure management. To mitigate these challenges, businesses should implement cost management strategies such as right-sizing, which involves selecting the appropriate VM size and configuration based on workload requirements. Cloud providers offer tools like AWS Cost Explorer, Azure Cost Management, and GCP's Billing Reports to help businesses monitor and optimize their cloud expenditures.

In addition to cost management, maintaining high availability and reliability is critical when scaling virtual machines in the cloud. As organizations scale their infrastructure to meet demand, they must ensure that the architecture remains resilient and can recover quickly from failures. High availability is often achieved by deploying VMs across multiple availability zones or regions within the cloud provider's infrastructure, ensuring that if one zone or region experiences an outage, traffic can be rerouted to other healthy instances. Load balancing plays a key role in this process, distributing traffic evenly across multiple VMs to prevent any single instance from becoming overwhelmed. In cloud environments, load balancing is typically automated, ensuring that the scaling process includes distributing the workload efficiently.

Another factor to consider when scaling virtual machines is the impact on networking. When additional VMs are provisioned or existing VMs are resized, network configurations must be adjusted to accommodate the new instances. This includes updating IP addresses, ensuring proper routing, and configuring network security policies to protect against unauthorized access. Cloud providers typically offer managed networking services that simplify these tasks, such as AWS Virtual Private Cloud (VPC), Azure Virtual Network, and GCP's Virtual Private Cloud. However, organizations still need to ensure that network configurations are optimized for scalability, security, and performance, particularly in multi-cloud or hybrid environments where cross-platform networking may be required.

Security is an ongoing concern when scaling virtual machines in cloud environments. As the infrastructure expands, it is essential to ensure that security policies and controls scale accordingly. This includes securing communication between VMs, ensuring that sensitive data is encrypted both in transit and at rest, and enforcing access control policies. Many cloud providers offer tools for automating security management, such as AWS Security Hub, Azure Security Center, and GCP's Security Command Center. These tools help administrators monitor security events, identify vulnerabilities, and enforce best practices for securing virtual machines at scale.

Scaling virtual machines in cloud environments enables organizations to respond dynamically to fluctuating workloads and ensure that applications perform optimally under varying levels of demand. The flexibility of cloud platforms allows businesses to scale their infrastructure both horizontally and vertically, optimizing resource utilization and maintaining high availability. However, effective scaling requires careful monitoring, performance analysis, and cost management to ensure that resources are provisioned appropriately and that the infrastructure remains resilient, secure, and cost-effective. By leveraging cloud automation tools, load balancing, and security management services, organizations can scale their virtual machines efficiently and meet the demands of an ever-changing business environment.

Virtual Machine Resource Limits and Throttling

In a virtualized environment, managing resources effectively is crucial for maintaining the performance, stability, and efficiency of the system. Virtual machines (VMs), as software-based representations of physical machines, rely on a shared pool of resources, including CPU, memory, storage, and network bandwidth. Since multiple VMs often run on a single physical host, each VM must be allocated a certain portion of the host's resources. Without proper control, resource contention can occur, leading to performance degradation, system instability, and inefficient use of hardware. Virtual machine resource limits and throttling are essential tools for ensuring that resources are distributed fairly and efficiently, preventing any single VM from monopolizing the host's resources and allowing other VMs to function properly.

Resource limits are configured in virtualized environments to define the maximum amount of resources that a virtual machine can consume. These limits are essential for controlling the behavior of VMs and ensuring that they do not exceed the available resources of the host machine. For example, CPU limits can be set to restrict how much processing power a VM can use, while memory limits ensure that a VM does not consume more RAM than is allocated. Disk and network resource limits can also be applied to control the amount of data a VM can read from or write to disk and the amount of network bandwidth it can consume. By setting these resource limits, administrators can prevent a single VM from overloading the system, ensuring that all VMs have fair access to the underlying hardware.

In addition to setting resource limits, virtual machine throttling is a technique used to regulate the consumption of resources when a VM reaches its assigned limits. Throttling refers to the intentional reduction of a VM's resource usage to prevent it from exceeding the allocated limits or to minimize the impact on other VMs running on the same host. Throttling can be applied to various resources, such as CPU, memory, disk I/O, and network bandwidth, to ensure that resource utilization remains within acceptable boundaries. For example, if a VM is consuming more CPU time than it should, throttling can reduce its processing power to allow other VMs to access the CPU. Similarly, if a VM is using too much network bandwidth, throttling can reduce its network speed to ensure that other VMs receive the necessary bandwidth.

The need for resource limits and throttling is particularly important in cloud computing environments, where virtualization is used to share a physical host's resources across many tenants. In a public or private cloud, multiple VMs from different users or departments may be hosted on the same physical server. Without proper resource allocation, one VM could consume an excessive amount of CPU, memory, or network bandwidth, negatively impacting the performance of other VMs. By enforcing resource limits and applying throttling policies, cloud providers can ensure that each tenant has fair access to the shared resources and that the overall performance of the system remains stable. These mechanisms help prevent resource hogging and ensure that the cloud infrastructure operates efficiently, even as the number of VMs and users grows.

Another important aspect of resource limits and throttling is the management of resource contention. When multiple VMs request resources at the same time, there may not be enough available to meet the demand. This can lead to performance issues, such as slow response times, increased latency, or even application failures. Resource contention is particularly common in environments with high workloads or when a large number of VMs are running on a single host. To address this, administrators can use resource scheduling and prioritization mechanisms to manage how resources are allocated during periods of contention. For instance, certain VMs may be prioritized based on their importance to the organization, ensuring that critical applications receive the necessary resources even when the host is under heavy load.

Resource limits and throttling also play a role in ensuring system stability and reliability. In a virtualized environment, resource spikes or excessive consumption by a single VM can destabilize the entire host, potentially affecting the performance of other VMs. Throttling prevents this by controlling the rate at which resources are allocated to each VM, reducing the likelihood of sudden surges in resource demand that could destabilize the system. This is particularly important in multi-tenant environments, where resource contention can have a broader impact. By proactively managing resource usage, throttling helps maintain the integrity of the system and ensures that all VMs operate within their resource limits, reducing the risk of crashes or slowdowns.

In addition to CPU, memory, and network resources, disk I/O management is also crucial in virtual machine resource allocation. Disk I/O is often a bottleneck in virtualized environments, as VMs can generate large amounts of read and write operations. If one VM consumes too much disk bandwidth, it can affect the performance of other VMs that need to access storage. By setting disk I/O limits and applying throttling, administrators can prevent a single VM from monopolizing the storage system, ensuring that all VMs have fair access to disk resources. Disk I/O throttling can be applied to both read and write operations, helping to maintain a balance between different VMs' demands on the storage system.

Virtual machine resource limits and throttling also play an essential role in optimizing the performance of virtualized environments. By effectively managing resources, administrators can ensure that VMs run at optimal performance levels without over-provisioning or under-provisioning resources. Over-provisioning occurs when VMs are allocated more resources than they need, which can lead to wasted resources and inefficiencies. Under-provisioning, on the other hand, can cause performance degradation and slow response times. By setting appropriate resource limits and applying throttling, administrators can strike a balance between providing enough resources for VMs to perform well and ensuring that those resources are used efficiently.

One of the key benefits of resource limits and throttling is the ability to maintain predictable performance in dynamic environments. Virtual machine workloads can vary significantly, with periods of high resource usage followed by periods of low activity. By dynamically adjusting resource allocation and applying throttling when necessary, administrators can ensure that the system remains stable and responsive, even during periods of fluctuating demand. This flexibility is essential in environments where workloads change rapidly, such as in cloud computing, data centers, or development and testing environments.

The implementation of resource limits and throttling also helps with cost optimization in cloud-based virtualized environments. Cloud providers typically charge customers based on the amount of resources consumed, such as CPU hours, memory usage, and bandwidth. By using resource limits and throttling, organizations can prevent the over-consumption of resources, ensuring that they only pay for the resources they actually need. This helps avoid unexpected costs and ensures that cloud resources are used efficiently, allowing businesses to optimize their infrastructure costs while maintaining the performance of their applications.

Virtual machine resource limits and throttling are essential tools for managing and optimizing virtualized environments. By controlling resource usage, preventing resource contention, and maintaining system stability, administrators can ensure that VMs operate efficiently and securely. Resource limits and throttling help optimize the performance of virtual machines, reduce operational costs, and ensure that resources are distributed fairly across multiple tenants or workloads. With the increasing reliance on virtualized infrastructure, these mechanisms are becoming more critical in ensuring the efficient and reliable operation of modern IT environments.

Monitoring Resource Utilization in Virtualized Environments

Monitoring resource utilization in virtualized environments is a critical aspect of managing virtual machines (VMs) and ensuring that the underlying infrastructure performs optimally. Virtualization allows multiple virtual machines to run on a single physical host, which brings efficiency and scalability to IT operations. However, it also introduces complexities in terms of resource management. Since multiple VMs share the same physical resources such as CPU, memory, storage, and network bandwidth, it is essential to track and monitor resource usage to prevent bottlenecks, ensure that resources are allocated appropriately, and maintain the performance and stability of both the virtual and physical layers of the infrastructure. Monitoring tools and techniques are crucial to achieving this goal, enabling administrators to track resource consumption in real-time, analyze trends, and take corrective actions when necessary.

In a virtualized environment, several types of resources need to be monitored to ensure smooth operation. The most important resources include CPU, memory, storage, and network bandwidth. CPU utilization in virtualized environments can be more complex to monitor than in physical environments because multiple VMs are competing for CPU cycles. If one VM consumes too many CPU resources, it can negatively affect the performance of other VMs on the same host. Monitoring CPU usage across all VMs allows administrators to identify whether any VM is overutilizing the CPU, which could result in resource contention, and adjust resource allocation as needed. By tracking CPU utilization, administrators can ensure that each VM receives the appropriate amount of processing power without overloading the system.

Memory usage is another key resource to monitor in virtualized environments. Each VM is allocated a certain amount of memory, but it can dynamically adjust based on the workload requirements. However, memory overcommitment is a common issue in virtualized systems, where more memory is allocated to VMs than the physical host can support. This can lead to swapping, where the system begins to use disk space as virtual memory, which can significantly degrade performance. Monitoring memory utilization helps ensure that each VM has sufficient memory allocated to meet its requirements without causing excessive swapping or memory contention. Additionally, administrators can use memory ballooning, a technique that dynamically adjusts memory allocation between VMs, to avoid overcommitment and optimize memory usage across the system.

Storage monitoring is also vital in virtualized environments, as virtual machines generate significant amounts of data that need to be stored and retrieved. Disk I/O performance can be a major bottleneck, especially in high-performance applications. When multiple VMs share the same physical storage, it is crucial to monitor disk usage and throughput to avoid saturation, which can lead to slow access times, system slowdowns, and potential failures. Monitoring tools can help administrators track disk performance, identify any storage bottlenecks, and take proactive measures to resolve issues before they affect the system. Storage optimization in virtualized environments often involves techniques such as deduplication, compression, and using SSDs to improve access times and overall performance.

Network bandwidth utilization is another critical area to monitor in virtualized environments. Since VMs often communicate with each other and with external systems, it is important to ensure that the network is not overloaded. Network congestion can lead to delays, packet loss, and degraded performance for all VMs sharing the network resources. Administrators must track the amount of data each VM is sending and receiving to identify any network traffic anomalies or overutilization. By monitoring network performance, administrators can optimize network traffic, prioritize critical workloads, and ensure that VMs are not competing for limited network resources. This monitoring is particularly important in environments with high network demands, such as those running databases, real-time applications, or web services.

Effective resource utilization monitoring also involves understanding the impact of workload changes on the performance of the virtualized infrastructure. As workloads fluctuate, resource consumption can change dynamically. For instance, during peak periods, certain VMs may require more CPU or memory, while others may require fewer resources. Monitoring tools can track these changes in real-time, enabling administrators to respond quickly to demand spikes. Additionally, by analyzing historical resource utilization data, administrators can identify patterns and make more accurate predictions about future resource needs. This data-driven approach allows for better capacity planning, ensuring that the infrastructure can scale appropriately to meet future demands without over-provisioning or underutilizing resources.

Cloud environments, in particular, benefit from resource utilization monitoring, as they provide highly dynamic and elastic infrastructure. Cloud platforms such as AWS, Microsoft Azure, and Google Cloud offer automatic scaling features, allowing resources to be added or removed based on demand. However, this scalability needs to be carefully managed to avoid unnecessary cost overruns or performance degradation. Monitoring tools help administrators track resource utilization in the cloud, enabling them to optimize scaling policies and ensure that VMs and other resources are provisioned appropriately. With the flexibility to scale up or down, cloud users must ensure that they are only paying for the resources they need, making accurate resource monitoring essential to controlling costs.

A key challenge in monitoring resource utilization in virtualized environments is ensuring visibility into both the virtual and physical layers. Virtualization adds a layer of abstraction between the VMs and the physical hardware, which can make it more difficult to obtain a clear view of resource usage across the entire system. Hypervisor management tools such as VMware vSphere, Microsoft Hyper-V, and KVM provide insights into resource allocation and usage at the VM level. However, for a comprehensive view of resource consumption, administrators need to integrate hypervisor-level monitoring with physical resource monitoring tools. This approach ensures that administrators have full visibility into how physical resources are being shared and used by the virtual machines, enabling better decision-making and resource optimization.

Automation plays a critical role in resource utilization monitoring, especially in large-scale virtualized environments. With the number of VMs and the complexity of modern infrastructures, manual monitoring is no longer practical. Automation tools can be configured to monitor resource usage continuously, identify potential issues, and even take corrective actions automatically. For example, if a VM is consistently consuming too much CPU or memory, an automated tool could scale the VM's resources, migrate it to a less heavily loaded host, or trigger an alert for manual intervention. Automation helps reduce the administrative burden of managing large virtualized environments and ensures that resources are allocated efficiently and in real-time.

In addition to monitoring tools, the use of analytics is increasingly important for optimizing resource utilization in virtualized environments. By leveraging machine learning and artificial intelligence (AI), modern monitoring systems can analyze resource usage patterns, identify inefficiencies, and predict future resource needs. This predictive capability allows organizations to proactively manage their virtualized infrastructure, scaling resources before issues arise and optimizing workloads for maximum efficiency. By applying advanced analytics to resource monitoring, administrators can improve the overall performance of the system while reducing operational costs.

Monitoring resource utilization in virtualized environments is essential for ensuring optimal performance, minimizing resource contention, and maintaining the overall health of the infrastructure. Effective monitoring allows administrators to track CPU, memory, storage, and network usage, ensuring that resources are allocated appropriately and efficiently. With the help of advanced monitoring tools, automation, and analytics, administrators can proactively manage their virtualized environments, respond to performance issues, and scale resources based on demand. As virtualized and cloud-based infrastructures continue to grow, the importance of resource utilization monitoring will only increase, helping organizations maximize the efficiency and effectiveness of their virtualized environments.

Virtual Machines in Hybrid Cloud Architectures

Virtual machines (VMs) are at the core of modern hybrid cloud architectures, providing the flexibility and scalability necessary for businesses to adapt to evolving workloads and IT requirements. Hybrid cloud environments, which combine on-premises infrastructure with public cloud resources, enable organizations to optimize their operations, increase agility, and manage costs effectively. By utilizing virtual machines within a hybrid cloud architecture, companies can leverage both private and public cloud resources to balance performance, security, and cost. The ability to dynamically allocate workloads between on-premises data centers and public cloud platforms makes hybrid clouds an attractive option for businesses looking to harness the benefits of cloud computing while maintaining control over sensitive data and critical applications.

In a hybrid cloud architecture, virtual machines offer an essential way to abstract and encapsulate workloads, making them portable between different environments. VMs can run on both private data centers and public cloud platforms, ensuring that applications are not locked into a single environment. This portability allows businesses to migrate workloads between the cloud and on-premises infrastructure as needed, facilitating smoother transitions, more efficient use of resources, and the ability to scale based on demand. For example, during peak usage periods, VMs can be migrated to public cloud infrastructure to take advantage of additional resources without the need to permanently expand on-premises hardware.

VMs in hybrid cloud environments also provide isolation and security, which is crucial when handling sensitive or regulated data. With hybrid cloud setups, organizations often need to ensure that sensitive workloads remain on-premises or in a private cloud to comply with security or regulatory requirements. At the same time, less critical workloads or applications that require more flexibility and scalability can be hosted in the public cloud. Virtual machines provide the necessary isolation between workloads by running separate operating systems and applications in isolated environments. This isolation ensures that sensitive data and critical applications can be safeguarded while allowing less sensitive tasks to take advantage of the cost-effectiveness and scalability of public cloud resources.

The flexibility of VMs allows for seamless workload migration across private and public cloud environments. Workloads that require high performance or low latency can remain on-premises, ensuring that they meet performance requirements without the inherent latency that may be introduced by cloud-based infrastructure. On the other hand, VMs running less resource-intensive applications can be deployed in the public cloud to take advantage of its elastic nature. This flexibility also enables disaster recovery and business continuity planning. In the event of an on-premises failure or disaster, workloads running on VMs can be quickly moved to the public cloud to ensure that critical services remain available. This hybrid approach to disaster recovery provides a cost-effective and efficient solution to maintaining uptime without requiring dedicated hardware for failover purposes.

In a hybrid cloud architecture, managing VMs becomes a key consideration for ensuring that resources are utilized efficiently and securely. Cloud management platforms such as VMware vSphere, Microsoft Azure, and AWS provide robust tools for managing virtual machines across hybrid environments. These platforms allow administrators to provision, monitor, and scale virtual machines with ease, ensuring that workloads are distributed appropriately between the public and private cloud. Additionally, automation tools can be employed to manage VM lifecycles, automate provisioning and scaling, and ensure that workloads are balanced effectively across both cloud environments. By using these management tools, businesses can optimize resource allocation, enhance scalability, and reduce the complexity of managing virtual machines in a hybrid cloud setup.

The performance of virtual machines in hybrid cloud environments is heavily dependent on network connectivity. Since workloads may span across both on-premises and cloud infrastructures, ensuring fast, reliable, and secure network connections is essential. The use of high-bandwidth, low-latency connections between private data centers and public clouds is critical for minimizing performance degradation during workload migration or when data needs to be shared between environments. Organizations often deploy dedicated virtual private networks (VPNs) or direct connection services, such as AWS Direct

Connect or Azure ExpressRoute, to ensure that their hybrid cloud infrastructure is connected with the necessary speed and security. Effective network management in hybrid cloud environments ensures that virtual machines can communicate across platforms seamlessly and that the infrastructure can scale without significant bottlenecks or latency issues.

Resource optimization is another key aspect of managing virtual machines in hybrid cloud environments. By running workloads in both private and public clouds, organizations can dynamically allocate resources based on current demand, ensuring that resources are not over-provisioned or underutilized. For example, during times of low demand, organizations can scale down VMs in the public cloud to save costs, while maintaining essential workloads on the private cloud. Conversely, during times of high demand, additional VMs can be spun up in the public cloud to handle the increased workload, and once the demand decreases, the resources can be scaled back. This ability to scale resources up and down in real time helps optimize costs while ensuring that performance requirements are met.

Despite the flexibility and scalability provided by virtual machines in hybrid cloud architectures, managing costs can be a challenge. While cloud providers offer the advantage of elastic scaling, the pay-as-you-go pricing model means that costs can quickly accumulate if resources are not properly managed. VMs that are left running when not needed or resources that are over-provisioned can lead to unnecessary expenses. To prevent this, organizations must implement cost management strategies, such as monitoring resource utilization, right-sizing VMs, and using automation to scale resources based on real-time demand. Cloud management tools and cost monitoring solutions offered by cloud providers can help organizations track and control their cloud spending, ensuring that they only pay for the resources they use.

Security remains one of the most significant concerns in hybrid cloud architectures, particularly when it comes to virtual machines. With workloads distributed across both public and private clouds, ensuring that data and applications are protected in transit and at rest is crucial. In hybrid environments, the risk of data breaches increases if proper security measures are not in place. Organizations must implement encryption for data at rest and in transit, ensure proper access control policies are enforced, and regularly audit and monitor virtual machines for security vulnerabilities. Cloud providers offer a range of security features, such as identity and access management (IAM), firewall services, and network isolation, to protect resources in hybrid environments. However, organizations are ultimately responsible for securing their virtual machines and ensuring compliance with relevant regulations and standards.

Virtual machines in hybrid cloud architectures offer organizations the flexibility to optimize their IT infrastructure, balancing performance, cost, and security. By taking advantage of both private and public cloud resources, businesses can scale workloads as needed, ensuring that critical applications remain performant while also leveraging the elasticity of the cloud for less critical tasks. Effective management of these virtual machines is essential for ensuring that resources are allocated efficiently, costs are controlled, and security risks are minimized. As hybrid cloud architectures continue to evolve, virtual machines will remain a cornerstone of scalable, flexible, and resilient IT infrastructure.

Performance Benchmarks for Virtualized Systems

Performance benchmarking for virtualized systems is essential for understanding the efficiency, responsiveness, and resource utilization of virtual machines (VMs) running on a hypervisor. As organizations increasingly rely on virtualization to consolidate workloads and optimize resource utilization, ensuring that virtual environments meet performance expectations is critical. Virtualization abstracts underlying hardware resources, and while this allows for flexibility and scalability, it also introduces complexity when it comes to managing performance. To ensure that virtualized systems deliver optimal results, performance benchmarks are used to measure how well these systems perform under different workloads and configurations. These benchmarks provide valuable insights into the effectiveness of the virtualized environment and help administrators make data-driven decisions for resource allocation, tuning, and troubleshooting.

One of the main challenges in virtualized environments is maintaining performance while balancing multiple workloads on the same physical hardware. In traditional physical setups, performance benchmarking tends to be more straightforward as the resources of the machine are dedicated to a single application or system. However, in a virtualized system, resources such as CPU, memory, and storage are shared across multiple virtual machines. This sharing can lead to resource contention, where multiple VMs compete for the same physical resources, potentially degrading the performance of all involved. Performance benchmarking for virtualized systems aims to measure how well the system manages this shared resource environment and ensures that each VM performs at an acceptable level.

Virtualization introduces overhead due to the hypervisor layer, which manages resource allocation and scheduling for VMs. This overhead, though necessary for enabling virtualization, can impact performance by introducing latency or reducing the processing power available to VMs. Performance benchmarks for virtualized systems often measure this overhead to determine the efficiency of the hypervisor and the impact it has on overall system performance. These benchmarks typically compare the performance of applications or workloads running on virtual machines with the performance of the same workloads on physical hardware. By measuring the difference in performance between virtual and physical environments, administrators can better understand the impact of the hypervisor and make adjustments to improve efficiency.

There are several key performance metrics that are measured during virtualized system benchmarking. CPU utilization is one of the most critical metrics, as CPU resources are often the primary constraint in virtualized environments. Virtual machines typically share CPU cores, and high CPU usage on one VM can affect the performance of other VMs on the same host. Benchmarking tools that track CPU utilization allow administrators to identify over-provisioned or under-provisioned VMs and adjust their resource allocation accordingly. Memory is another vital resource that needs to be monitored, especially in systems where memory overcommitment is common. Monitoring memory usage ensures that VMs do not consume more resources than are available, preventing issues like excessive swapping or memory ballooning, which can degrade performance. Additionally, storage performance is a key benchmark, particularly in environments with high data throughput requirements. Disk I/O performance can be a bottleneck in virtualized environments, and measuring disk read/write speeds and latencies is crucial to understanding how well the system handles data access. Finally, network performance is often a critical factor in virtualized systems, especially in environments with high network traffic. Benchmarking network throughput, latency, and packet loss helps administrators ensure that VMs can communicate efficiently within the virtualized infrastructure.

Benchmarking tools are essential for obtaining accurate and reliable performance data. Many benchmarking tools are specifically designed for virtualized environments, allowing administrators to simulate different workloads and capture performance metrics across a range of system configurations. Tools such as PassMark, SPECvirt, and Vdbench are commonly used for performance testing in virtual environments. These tools can simulate real-world applications, generating workloads that stress various system components, including CPU, memory, storage, and network. By running these tools in both virtual and physical environments, administrators can assess the impact of virtualization on system performance and identify any potential issues related to resource contention, hypervisor overhead, or configuration problems. Additionally, cloud-based tools like Amazon Web Services' CloudWatch and Microsoft Azure Monitor can be used to benchmark virtualized systems in public cloud environments, providing valuable insights into how well virtual machines perform in a cloud-based infrastructure.

In addition to assessing the performance of individual VMs, benchmarking virtualized systems involves evaluating the overall performance of the entire virtualized infrastructure. This includes measuring the efficiency of the hypervisor in managing resource allocation, balancing workloads, and handling resource contention. Hypervisor performance can significantly impact the performance of virtual machines, and benchmarking can reveal areas where the hypervisor's resource management can be improved. For example, hypervisors often use techniques like CPU scheduling and memory ballooning to allocate resources to VMs. Benchmarking can reveal how well these techniques work in practice and identify opportunities for optimization. Load balancing within a virtualized environment is another key area that can be assessed through performance benchmarking. By distributing workloads evenly across available resources, load balancing helps prevent any single VM or host from becoming overwhelmed, improving overall system performance.

The results of performance benchmarks are crucial for making informed decisions about resource allocation, VM configurations, and system tuning. By identifying performance bottlenecks, administrators can adjust the allocation of CPU, memory, and storage resources to improve overall system efficiency. For example, if a benchmark reveals that a particular VM is consuming excessive CPU resources, the administrator might choose to reduce the number of vCPUs allocated to that VM or move it to a host with more available CPU capacity. Similarly, if disk I/O is identified as a bottleneck, administrators might optimize the storage configuration or move the affected VM to a different storage device with higher throughput capabilities. In cloud environments, performance benchmarks can also help organizations determine the most cost-effective virtual machine configurations. By benchmarking different VM sizes and configurations, businesses can optimize their cloud infrastructure to ensure that they are getting the best performance for the lowest cost.

Another important aspect of performance benchmarking for virtualized systems is ensuring that VMs are appropriately sized for their workloads. Over-provisioning, where a VM is allocated more resources than it needs, can lead to inefficiencies and wasted resources, while under-provisioning can result in poor performance and resource starvation. Benchmarking helps identify the optimal resource allocation for each VM, ensuring that it has enough resources to perform well without overburdening the host or wasting valuable infrastructure resources. This approach is particularly important in cloud environments, where businesses often pay for resources based on usage. Properly sized VMs ensure that organizations are not over-paying for unnecessary resources while still meeting performance requirements.

Performance benchmarking also plays a vital role in identifying areas for system optimization. By analyzing performance data, administrators can pinpoint areas of inefficiency or suboptimal configurations. For example, if disk I/O performance is found to be slower than expected, administrators may consider using different storage solutions, such as solid-state drives (SSDs), or reconfiguring the storage network to improve access times. Similarly, if network performance is a bottleneck, network configuration adjustments or the use of more advanced network hardware may be required. Benchmarking results can guide these optimization efforts, helping organizations make data-driven decisions to improve performance, reduce costs, and enhance the overall user experience.

Performance benchmarks for virtualized systems are essential for understanding the behavior of virtual machines in a shared resource environment. These benchmarks provide valuable insights into how virtualized systems handle workloads and resource contention, helping administrators identify bottlenecks, optimize resource allocation, and ensure that VMs perform efficiently. By using benchmarking tools to simulate real-world applications and workloads, administrators can assess the impact of virtualization on system performance and take steps to mitigate any performance issues. Whether in private data centers or public cloud environments, performance benchmarking is a key practice for ensuring that virtualized systems meet the needs of modern business operations.

Migrating Virtual Machines to New Hypervisors

Migrating virtual machines (VMs) to new hypervisors is an essential task for organizations looking to optimize their infrastructure, take advantage of new technologies, or reduce costs. As businesses grow and their virtualization needs evolve, it often becomes necessary to transition VMs from one hypervisor to another. This migration can be driven by various factors, including the desire for better performance, improved scalability, or cost savings through more efficient virtualization platforms. Regardless of the reasons, migrating virtual machines to new hypervisors is a complex process that requires careful planning, proper tools, and an understanding of the potential challenges involved. Successfully migrating VMs ensures that workloads remain accessible, secure, and efficient in the new environment, without causing significant downtime or disruption to business operations.

The first step in migrating virtual machines to a new hypervisor is understanding the differences between the existing and target hypervisors. Hypervisors vary in terms of architecture, capabilities, and compatibility with different guest operating systems. For instance, VMware vSphere, Microsoft Hyper-V, and KVM are widely used hypervisors, each with its own set of features and management tools. Before migrating, it is crucial to ensure that the target hypervisor supports the same virtual machine configurations, including the operating systems and applications running on the VMs. In some cases, certain VMs may need to be reconfigured or updated to be compatible with the new hypervisor. Additionally, understanding the underlying infrastructure requirements of the new hypervisor is essential for ensuring that the physical hardware meets the necessary specifications and performance expectations.

Once the compatibility of the virtual machines and the target hypervisor has been confirmed, the next step involves selecting the right migration method. Several methods can be used to migrate VMs between hypervisors, depending on the level of compatibility between the source and destination platforms. If both hypervisors support common formats, such as the Open Virtualization Format (OVF), migration can be relatively straightforward. The OVF format is a widely accepted standard for packaging and distributing virtual machines, and it allows VMs to be exported from one hypervisor and imported into another with minimal changes. However, not all hypervisors natively support OVF, and in those cases, other migration tools or methods may need to be used.

In some situations, organizations may use a hypervisor migration tool or platform designed to handle cross-hypervisor migrations. These tools simplify the migration process by automating many of the tasks involved, including the conversion of virtual disk formats, reconfiguration of virtual hardware, and synchronization of VM settings. For example, VMware vCenter Converter is a popular tool that allows users to migrate VMs from different hypervisors, including Microsoft Hyper-V and VMware, to the vSphere platform. Similarly, tools like Microsoft Virtual Machine Converter (MVMC) enable the migration of VMs from VMware to Hyper-V. These tools streamline the migration process and reduce the risk of errors, making it easier for administrators to move VMs between hypervisors while maintaining consistency and minimizing downtime.

Another option for migrating virtual machines between hypervisors is live migration, which allows VMs to be moved from one hypervisor to another with minimal downtime. Live migration is particularly useful in environments where downtime must be minimized, such as in production environments or when high availability is critical. However, live migration requires specific capabilities, such as shared storage between the source and target hypervisors, and may not be supported by all hypervisors or configurations. In cases where live migration is not possible, administrators can perform a cold migration, which involves shutting down the VM, migrating the virtual disk files, and reconfiguring the VM on the new hypervisor before powering it back on. While cold migrations tend to result in longer downtime, they may be necessary if live migration is not supported or if the VM is not configured for live migration.

Before performing the migration, administrators must also consider the network configurations of the virtual machines. Network settings, such as virtual switches, network adapters, and IP addresses, must be reviewed and adjusted to ensure that VMs function correctly in the new hypervisor environment. In some cases, network drivers may need to be updated to match the requirements of the new hypervisor. Additionally, any virtual networking configurations, such as VLANs or firewall rules, should be carefully examined to ensure compatibility with the target hypervisor. Network configuration issues can lead to communication failures between virtual machines and other systems, so thorough testing is essential after the migration process.

Storage is another critical factor in the migration process. Different hypervisors may use different virtual disk formats, which could result in compatibility issues during the migration. For instance, VMware uses the VMDK format for virtual disks, while Hyper-V uses VHD or

VHDX formats. In many cases, it may be necessary to convert the virtual disk format to match the target hypervisor. This can be done using specialized disk conversion tools, which will allow the VM's virtual hard drive to be compatible with the new hypervisor. Additionally, administrators must ensure that storage configurations, such as disk provisioning (thin vs. thick), are appropriately adjusted to avoid performance issues after migration. Storage performance can be affected during the migration process, so testing the virtual machine's disk I/O performance after migration is essential to ensure that it continues to meet the required performance standards.

Once the migration process has been completed, administrators should thoroughly test the virtual machine to ensure that it is functioning correctly in the new hypervisor environment. This testing should include verifying that the VM boots properly, confirming that all applications are working as expected, and checking that network connectivity is intact. Additionally, administrators should monitor the VM's resource utilization, such as CPU, memory, and disk usage, to ensure that the virtual machine is operating efficiently. Any discrepancies in resource allocation or performance can be addressed by adjusting the VM's configuration or optimizing the underlying hypervisor settings.

One of the final steps in the migration process involves decommissioning the old virtual machine or deactivating it on the previous hypervisor. It is important to ensure that the original VM is properly removed from the source hypervisor to prevent resource duplication and avoid any security risks. Administrators should also update any monitoring and management systems to reflect the new location of the virtual machine, ensuring that it is monitored appropriately in the new environment.

The migration of virtual machines to new hypervisors is a process that requires careful planning and execution. While the benefits of migrating VMs, such as improved performance, cost savings, and enhanced scalability, are significant, the migration process can be complex and challenging. By understanding the compatibility requirements, selecting the right migration tools, ensuring proper network and storage configurations, and thoroughly testing the VMs post-migration, administrators can ensure a smooth transition to the new hypervisor environment. The ability to migrate VMs across hypervisors provides organizations with the flexibility to adapt their virtualization infrastructure as needs evolve, making it a key capability in modern IT environments.

Future Trends in Virtualization and VM Management

As virtualization continues to evolve, the way virtual machines (VMs) are managed and utilized is undergoing significant transformation. The future of virtualization is shaped by several key trends that are being driven by advancements in technology, changing business needs, and the growing demands of cloud computing, artificial intelligence (AI), and automation. These trends promise to enhance the flexibility, efficiency, and scalability of virtualized environments, making them even more integral to modern IT infrastructures. Virtualization is no longer just about consolidating hardware resources; it is now a cornerstone of cloud-native architectures, hybrid environments, and AI-driven automation.

One of the most significant trends in the future of virtualization is the increasing adoption of containerization alongside traditional virtual machines. While VMs have long been a standard for creating isolated computing environments, containers have emerged as a lighter-weight alternative that offers speed and efficiency, particularly for microservices-based applications. Containers allow for rapid deployment and scaling, with less overhead than traditional VMs, which makes them an attractive option for developers working in agile environments. The rise of Kubernetes and container orchestration platforms is further driving this trend, as organizations seek to modernize their applications and infrastructure. However, VMs will continue to play a vital role in the future, especially for workloads that require complete isolation, legacy applications, or specialized operating systems. The future of virtualization will likely involve more integration between VMs and containers, with hybrid environments that leverage the strengths of both technologies to meet the varying demands of different workloads.

The increasing importance of hybrid and multi-cloud environments is another trend that is shaping the future of virtualization. As organizations continue to embrace the cloud for its scalability and flexibility, many are also maintaining on-premises infrastructure for specific use cases, such as regulatory compliance or legacy application support. This hybrid approach requires advanced virtualization technologies that can span across both private and public clouds, enabling seamless management of virtual machines across multiple environments. The future of VM management will likely focus on providing integrated solutions that allow administrators to manage VMs regardless of whether they reside on-premises, in the public cloud, or in hybrid configurations. This integration will include centralized management tools, unified dashboards, and cross-cloud capabilities that simplify the deployment, monitoring, and scaling of VMs across different platforms.

In parallel with these trends, advancements in automation and artificial intelligence (AI) will play a significant role in the future of VM management. Traditionally, managing VMs and virtualized environments has required considerable manual intervention, particularly when it comes to provisioning, scaling, and troubleshooting. However, AI and machine learning algorithms are increasingly being used to automate many aspects of VM management, such as resource allocation, load balancing, and performance optimization. AI-powered tools can analyze large volumes of performance data to predict future resource needs and dynamically adjust VM configurations to meet changing demands. This level of automation will not only reduce the administrative burden on IT teams but also improve the overall efficiency and responsiveness of virtualized environments. As AI-driven automation continues to mature, it will enable self-healing systems that can automatically detect and resolve issues without human intervention, further improving uptime and reliability.

The growth of edge computing is another trend that will impact the future of virtualization. As more devices become connected to the internet, there is a growing need to process data closer to the source to reduce latency and improve response times. This has led to the rise of edge computing, where computing resources are distributed across a network of edge nodes, such as local data centers or even devices themselves. Virtualization will play a crucial role in the expansion of edge computing by enabling lightweight, distributed virtual machines that can run on edge devices. These virtual machines will be responsible for processing and analyzing data in real time, without relying on a centralized data center. The future of virtualization will involve the development of more efficient, low-latency virtual machine technologies that can operate in these distributed, resource-constrained environments, enabling new use cases in areas like IoT, autonomous vehicles, and smart cities.

Another important trend shaping the future of virtualization is the growing focus on security. As virtualized environments become more complex and widely used, securing virtual machines and the infrastructure they run on is becoming increasingly critical. Traditional security models, which were designed for physical environments, are no longer sufficient to protect modern virtualized systems. In the future, VM security will need to be more integrated into the virtualization layer itself, with enhanced capabilities for isolating workloads, monitoring traffic, and detecting threats in real time. New technologies, such as hardware-assisted virtualization security and secure enclave technologies, are already beginning to make their way into virtualized environments, providing a higher level of protection for sensitive data and workloads. Additionally, security automation and AI will be used to identify vulnerabilities, automate patch management, and provide real-time incident response, making it easier to protect virtual machines against increasingly sophisticated cyber threats.

As organizations continue to demand more scalable and efficient IT infrastructures, the future of virtualization will also be driven by innovations in resource management and optimization. Modern virtualized systems need to be able to dynamically adjust resources to meet the demands of a wide variety of workloads. Virtualization platforms are increasingly being designed to support real-time, elastic resource allocation, enabling VMs to scale up or down based on workload requirements. This will be particularly important as cloud environments grow, with virtual machines needing to quickly adapt to changing demand patterns. Future virtualization technologies will likely focus on optimizing the use of physical resources, reducing wastage, and improving the overall cost-effectiveness of virtualized infrastructures.

The integration of serverless computing is also becoming a key consideration in the future of virtualization. Serverless computing allows developers to run code in response to events without provisioning or managing servers. This abstraction eliminates the need to manually manage VMs, making it an attractive option for developers who want to focus on building applications rather than managing infrastructure. However, while serverless computing eliminates the need for traditional server management, virtualization will still play a role in providing the underlying infrastructure. Virtual machines will likely be used in the background to support serverless environments, and virtualization technologies will evolve to seamlessly integrate with serverless platforms, ensuring efficient resource management and scalability.

Lastly, with the rise of containerized environments, the future of virtualization will likely include advancements in container and VM integration. While containers offer efficiency and speed, virtual machines provide greater isolation and full operating systems. The future will see more hybrid environments where containers and VMs coexist, with orchestration tools that allow for seamless interaction between the two. This integration will allow organizations to benefit from the strengths of both containers and virtual machines, creating a more flexible, scalable, and efficient IT infrastructure that can handle a wide range of workloads and applications.

The future of virtualization and VM management is exciting and full of promise. As technology continues to evolve, virtualization will play an even more critical role in enabling organizations to meet the demands of modern IT environments. From hybrid cloud architectures to AI-driven automation, edge computing, and enhanced security, the trends shaping the future of virtualization will provide new opportunities for businesses to improve efficiency, reduce costs, and innovate. The continued development of virtualization technologies will help organizations build more resilient, scalable, and secure infrastructures that can keep pace with the rapidly changing digital landscape.

Best Practices for Virtual Machine Management

Effective management of virtual machines (VMs) is essential for maintaining optimal performance, security, and efficiency in virtualized environments. Virtual machines, which allow organizations to run multiple isolated workloads on a single physical server, are central to modern IT infrastructure. However, managing these VMs requires careful planning, consistent monitoring, and best practices to ensure that resources are used effectively and that systems remain secure and scalable. By following industry best practices, administrators can optimize VM performance, minimize downtime, and reduce the complexity of managing virtualized environments.

One of the most important best practices for virtual machine management is ensuring proper resource allocation. Virtual machines share the physical resources of the host system, including CPU, memory, storage, and network bandwidth. Misallocating resources can lead to performance bottlenecks, resource contention, and system instability. It is crucial to correctly allocate CPU, memory, and storage to each VM based on the workload requirements. Over-provisioning resources can lead to inefficiencies, while under-provisioning may cause performance degradation. Administrators should regularly review resource utilization and adjust the allocations as needed to maintain balance across all VMs. In dynamic environments, automated resource allocation and scaling can help ensure that resources are assigned optimally based on demand.

Another critical best practice is maintaining up-to-date backup and disaster recovery plans. Virtual machines are susceptible to data loss or corruption, whether due to hardware failure, human error, or malicious attacks. Regular backups of VM images and critical data are essential to ensure that systems can be quickly restored in the event of a failure. Administrators should implement automated backup solutions that take regular snapshots of VMs, storing these backups in secure locations, such as off-site storage or the cloud. Disaster recovery plans should also include VM replication to remote locations, allowing VMs to be restored quickly and with minimal downtime. Testing these backup and recovery processes regularly ensures that they will function as expected when needed.

Security is another top priority in VM management, as virtualized environments are particularly vulnerable to threats due to their shared nature. Ensuring proper security configurations is essential to protect the virtualized infrastructure from unauthorized access, data breaches, and attacks. One best practice is to implement network segmentation, using virtual networks or VLANs to isolate VMs from each other and from the external network. This helps prevent unauthorized lateral movement within the infrastructure. Additionally, administrators should configure firewalls, intrusion detection systems, and security policies on both the virtual machines and the host system. Regular patching and updating of both the hypervisor and the guest operating systems are also crucial to ensure that vulnerabilities are addressed promptly.

Virtual machine monitoring is an essential part of effective VM management. By continuously monitoring VM performance, administrators can identify and resolve issues before they escalate into major problems. Tools that provide real-time visibility into CPU, memory, disk, and network usage help administrators detect performance bottlenecks and resource contention. Performance monitoring should also include tracking VM uptime, load balancing, and resource utilization trends over time. Proactive monitoring allows administrators to fine-tune resource allocation, ensure that VMs are performing optimally, and prevent system failures that could disrupt business operations. Additionally, implementing automated alerts for abnormal behavior or resource usage ensures that administrators can respond quickly to potential issues.

Another best practice is to automate as much of the virtual machine management process as possible. Automation reduces human error, enhances efficiency, and enables more agile management of virtualized environments. Tasks such as provisioning, scaling, and patching can be automated using orchestration tools and scripts. This allows administrators to deploy new VMs quickly, adjust resources dynamically based on workload demands, and apply updates across multiple VMs without manual intervention. Automation also plays a key role in compliance management, as administrators can configure policies that ensure VMs are consistently deployed with the correct configurations, security settings, and patches.

Effective VM lifecycle management is another important aspect of virtual machine best practices. The lifecycle of a VM includes several stages: creation, deployment, monitoring, maintenance, and retirement. Administrators should follow standardized processes for each of these stages to ensure consistency and efficiency. For example, during the creation and deployment phase, administrators should use templates and predefined configurations to ensure that VMs are set up correctly and consistently. During the maintenance phase, administrators should perform routine tasks such as updating software, checking for performance degradation, and optimizing VM configurations. When a VM reaches the end of its useful life, it should be decommissioned and deleted properly to free up resources and ensure that sensitive data is securely removed.

Capacity planning is another critical best practice for virtual machine management. As organizations grow and their infrastructure needs evolve, it is essential to plan for future resource requirements. Administrators should analyze historical usage patterns, monitor current resource utilization, and project future demand to ensure that the virtualized environment can scale as needed. This includes evaluating hardware requirements, planning for additional storage, and ensuring that there is enough compute power to handle increasing workloads. A well-executed capacity planning strategy helps prevent resource shortages and ensures that the virtualized infrastructure can meet the needs of the business without unnecessary over-provisioning.

VM migration is another key aspect of VM management. In many cases, workloads need to be moved between hosts or even between different data centers to balance resources, improve performance, or support business continuity efforts. Best practices for VM migration include planning migrations carefully to minimize downtime and disruptions. Administrators should test migrations in non-production environments to identify potential issues before performing them in a live environment. Additionally, it is important to ensure that storage and networking configurations are adjusted as necessary during the migration process to prevent issues with connectivity or data access.

Automating the migration process can also reduce the likelihood of errors and improve the efficiency of moving workloads.

Documentation and record-keeping are also vital to successful virtual machine management. Maintaining up-to-date records of all VMs, their configurations, and associated resources allows administrators to manage the environment more effectively. Documentation should include details about each VM's purpose, resource allocations, operating systems, applications, and security configurations. This information is critical for troubleshooting, audits, and compliance purposes. Administrators should also document any changes made to the virtualized environment, including updates, migrations, and resource reallocations, to ensure transparency and maintain a historical record of decisions and configurations.

Finally, integrating virtual machine management with other IT operations, such as network and storage management, helps create a cohesive and efficient virtualized environment. VM management should be aligned with the overall infrastructure strategy, and administrators should work closely with other teams to ensure that network configurations, storage resources, and backup solutions are properly integrated with the virtualized environment. This collaboration ensures that virtual machines are supported by a robust and well-managed infrastructure, minimizing the risk of performance issues or downtime.

Following these best practices for virtual machine management helps ensure that virtualized environments run smoothly, efficiently, and securely. From resource allocation to security, monitoring, automation, and lifecycle management, administrators must take a comprehensive approach to VM management to meet the needs of modern IT infrastructures. By applying these best practices, organizations can optimize their virtualized systems, minimize downtime, and improve the overall performance of their IT environments. Effective VM management not only enhances operational efficiency but also enables businesses to scale and adapt to new technologies and demands.

www.ingramcontent.com/pod-product-compliance
Lightning Source LLC
LaVergne TN
LVHW022314060326
832902LV00020B/3455